Change Your Brainwaves – Change Your Karma

Nichiren Buddhism 3.1

Susanne Matsudo-Kiliani &
Yukio Matsudo

COPYRIGHT AND DISCLAIMER

© 2017 Yukio Matsudo & Susanne Matsudo-Kiliani

This edition was published in August 2017 by DPI Publishing, Heidelberg, Germany.

https://www.facebook.com/DPIpublishing/

All rights reserved. No part of this publication may be reproduced
by any mechanical, photographic or electronic process,
or in the form of phonographic recording;
nor may it be stored in a retrieval system, transmitted
or otherwise be copied for public or private use,
other than for 'fair use' as brief quotations embodied in articles and reviews, without prior permission in writing of the author.

The information given in this book should not be treated
as a substitute for professional therapeutic or medical advice.
Any use of information in this book is at the reader's discretion and risk.
Neither the author nor the publisher can be held responsible
for any loss, claim or damage arising out of use, or misuse,
of the suggestions made, the failure to take therapeutic or medical advice or for any material on third party websites.

ISBN 978-1974345236

Contents

Foreword — 9

Chapter 1
The fascinating aspects of Nichiren Buddhism — 13

Looking for a Buddhist practice — 13
Part of my family karma — 14
Did you inherit your grandma´s emotions? — 15
We are not at the mercy of our genes — 16
Is life just happening to you? — 17
My encounter with Nichiren Buddhism — 18
Being enchanted while chanting — 19
Could that really be true? — 20
Chanting to realize specific wishes — 21
Chanting daimoku dissolves old blockages — 22
Transform your own negativity — 23
The mystic coincidence of synchronicity — 23
The event will find you — 25

Chapter 2
Facing your blockages — 28

Becoming aware of your emotional blockages — 28
Becoming true to yourself — 30
Different strategies to cope with fear — 30
This or something better — 31
To what extent do you see yourself as a victim? — 34
What is your victim story? — 35
Where is your attention going? — 36
The old must make room for the new — 38

Chapter 3
Consciousness is energy — **41**

Our thoughts are real forces	41
The intention of peace creates peace	42
Sending love to water	43
The power of intention has no limit	45
Others know what you are feeling	47
Thought forms are tangible energy	49
Your negative intention may become reality	50
The Gohonzon as an amplifier of our thoughts and feelings	52
Become crystal clear about what you want	53
Can you measure your state of mind?	54

Chapter 4
Can we measure the transformation? — **56**

Can you measure the effects of daimoku?	56
Our first measurement attempts	57
An astonishing measurement result	59
Does daimoku change your brainwaves?	61
What are brainwaves?	62
Gamma brainwaves: learning and storing new information	63
Beta brainwaves: from focus to anxiety	64
Highest levels of focus	*64*
To be effective in everyday consciousness	*64*
High beta: stress and fear in everyday consciousness	*65*
You are thinking too much	*65*
Alpha-brainwaves: relaxation and clarity of mind	66
Relax your body and clear your mind	*66*
When you are in the flow with daimoku	*67*
Theta brainwaves: reprogram your subconscious	67
Be more creative	*68*
Reprogram your subconscious mind	*68*
Neutralize old traumatic experiences	*69*
Delta brainwaves: healing and spiritual connection	69
Rejuvenate yourself	*69*

Anti-aging effects	70
Increased compassion and intuition	70
The deepest level of mind	70
Connecting with universal life energy	71
The goal of advanced meditation	71

Chapter 5
Shift your brainwave frequency with daimoku   73

What changes occur during daimoku?	73
What is an QEEG?	73
What is brain mapping?	74
Measurement before chanting daimoku	75
Train your brain fitness	77
Measuring brainwaves during daimoku meditation	77
What is brain coherence?	79
A state of deep transformation	80
Your brain is like a sponge	*81*
Program your reality in theta	*82*
Solve your problems in theta	*83*
Transform your emotions in theta	*83*
Heal yourself in theta	*83*
Transform your blockages and beliefs	84
Get access to unlimited pure consciousness	85
Connect to the source of all being	86
How do you know whether you are connected or not?	87

Chapter 6
Brain synchronization with daimoku   88

Coherence is the magic word	88
Balancing the left and right brain hemispheres	89
Your critical mind and your creative mind	91
When you are out of sync	93
When your brainwaves are out of sync	94
An incoherent brain makes you ill	95
An incoherent brain causes stress and depression	95

A coherent brain – the necessary condition for healing	96
Do you feel overwhelmed?	*97*
You are getting a wider perspective on things	*97*
You are able to detect patterns	*98*
Brainwave synchronization with daimoku	99
Improve your emotional stability	*100*
You get attracted to different situations	*100*
Be more relaxed about things	*101*
The anti-aging effects of daimoku	*102*
The secret to being successful	103
A synchronized brain makes you a good leader	103
Transform fear and worry	106
When does your amygdala get activated?	106
Fear stops your motivation	*109*
Avoid amygdala attacks	*109*
Calm your fear center	*110*
Relax your monkey mind	111
Itai dōshin, or, to be in harmony with yourself	112
Dōtai ishin is an incoherent state	*112*

Chapter 7
Consciousness is multi-dimensional — 115

Is consciousness a product of the brain?	115
Beyond your brain	116
A journey to non-local consciousness	117
Your Buddha nature corresponds to non-local consciousness	119
Karma creates your individual way of life	121
The light behind it all	122

Chapter 8
The Buddhist deep psychology of karma — 125

You think you decide consciously	125
Your subconscious mind controls everything	127
We are looking for solutions on the outside	128
Your ego-identity is defined by external stimuli	129

A Buddhist multilayer model of consciousness	131
You are controlled by your karmic patterns	133
What beliefs are running your life?	134
Daimoku makes you aware of your karmic tendencies	138
Case study 1: The unpleasant effect of my helper syndrome	138
Case study 2: Anna missed the chance of her life	140

Chapter 9
Collective karma affecting your life — 144

The eighth level: The storehouse of your karma	144
The cultural categories in your mind	145
Family karma	147
Case Study 3: Part of my family karma	148
Case Study 4: A deep passion for flamenco	149
The informational patterns of past generations	150
Your karmic tendencies always influence your life	152
Case study 5: An inconsistent way of living	155
A fatalistic view of karmic retribution	156
Your autopilot mechanism makes you a victim	158
Case study 6: Petra's disappointment	158
Repeating the same experience again and again	160

Chapter 10
The karma free zone of pure consciousness — 163

The ninth consciousness is within you	163
Overcoming your self-centeredness	164
Nichiren's Buddhism of the shining sun	166
You start by activating non-local consciousness	169
Don't confuse outer reality with the source	171
"Slander" is to deny the dignity of your life	172
Ichinen Sanzen represents this basic principle	175

Chapter 11
Your subconscious mind is in your body — 177

Why is karma so persistent?	177

Karma is stored on a cellular level	179
Karma in terms of emotional energy	180
We are addicted to certain emotions	181
Case study 7: To stop smoking	182
Being addicted to a certain way of thinking	184
Daimoku releases your stored emotions	186
Disrupt your emotional addictions	189

Chapter 12
The neuroscience of karma — 191

Your karma is stored in your neural networks	191
Release old traumatic experiences	192
Neurons that fire together wire together	193
The powerful patterns of your emotional reactions	194
The emotional content of your memories	195
Case study 8: Projecting old experiences to the present	195
Your brain is a record of your past	196

Chapter 13
Daimoku is a powerful pattern breaker — 198

Daimoku interrupts emotional addictions	198
Brainwave measurement while chanting together	201
The clinical application of the alpha-theta crossover	203
Your intention is already realized	205
From alpha to theta to delta	205
Emotionally living in the future	206
Polishing your mirror day and night	209

Bibliography — 211

About the authors — 214

Foreword

"No problem can be solved from the same level of consciousness that created it." With this statement Albert Einstein linked the way that we experience reality to the state of our consciousness. At the same time he indicated that there are different levels of reality that are associated with different levels of consciousness. Thus, if you want to change your outer situation – the way you feel and act or what situations you become attracted to in life – you first have to change your current level of consciousness.

In 2010 Daisaku Ikeda discussed the relationship between religion and science in a dialogue with the Japanese neuroscientist Ken'ichiro Mogi. In this dialogue Ikeda took the firm position that religion and science should not be treated as separate from each other, nor should they remain in a conflict relationship. Instead, they should complement and mutually benefit each other. We would like to follow Ikeda's constructive and value-creating approach by presenting in this book our attempt to build a bridge between the wisdom of Nichiren Buddhism and the knowledge of modern science.

In our first book of the series *Nichiren Buddhism 3.0* we considered Nichiren Buddhist concepts and principles mainly in terms of "energy". In this respect we measured the positive effects of daimoku on our own body and on our own energy centers (chakras) as well as the energetic effects on our own energy field. We also measured the energy in the room where we were chanting.

In this book, *Nichiren Buddhism 3.1*, we take a closer look at the effects of daimoku in terms of "consciousness". Once again we are dealing with energy, since consciousness can also be regarded as energy because it is related to our brain activity, which can be measured in the form of vibration and frequency. We will show the results of our brainwave measurements taken whilst chanting **daimoku**.

In this regard, we discovered an interesting correspondence between the levels of consciousness taught in Nichiren Buddhism and the frequencies of our brainwaves.

Our measurements have shown that practicing **daimoku** enables us to experience the state of *brain synchronization*. This is a kind of brain state that neuroscientists have long associated with creating a natural balance between your mind and your body, with radiant health, greater wellbeing, successful leadership and the kind of energy that really gets you motivated.

Find out how and why the practice of **daimoku** is linked to your personal success and how it can be an essential help in achieving your desired goals in life.

In this respect, you will find some neuroscientific explanations about the positive effects of **daimoku** such as making you vital and younger, getting more mental clarity, giving you confidence and emotional stability, helping you to overcome stress and depression, and finally allowing you to enter a deep spiritual connection that is required to change your karmic tendencies.

You might have often observed that many people keep repeating the same patterns over and over again and always end up in the same problematic situation accompanied by the same way of feeling and thinking. They might change their job, but end up with the same kind of boss or in the same stressful environment. They might change their partner but always end up having the same kind of arguments. They might be able to get more money but always end up being bankrupt at a much higher level than before. How can we interrupt this vicious cycle and get out of the hamster wheel?

In this context we considered the questions: How can you explain and change karma in a neuroscientific way? Is your karma stored on a physical level?

In this regard, we were also dealing with the fundamental problem of fear that everyone is confronted with, since fear and other negative emotions like anger and insecurity function as a real emotional blockage, stopping you from achieving your goals. A person needs to break through these negative emotions that are deeply stored in their subconscious mind to put their desired vision into reality.

Based on our brainwave measurements, this book demonstrates that chanting daimoku is a real and effective PATTERN BREAKER of negative emotions, limiting beliefs and burdening karmic patterns and tendencies that have been passed down in our genetic lines for generations. It even seems to be much more effective than many neuro-feedback therapies that have been developed to treat certain dysfunctional symptoms on a neuro-physiological level.

Many people invest a lot of money, energy and time solely in physical fitness, a healthy diet and nutritional supplements. However, your state of health, your emotional wellbeing, your relationship with yourself and with others, even your success and your happiness in life, are fundamentally linked to the deeper level of your life state and to how your mind functions.

Therefore we must invest at least as much time in our brain fitness as we may spend in physical fitness. Chanting daimoku can serve you as such a basis for improving your wellbeing in your brain and your body.

The results of our scientific research are illustrated with many personal experiences, in order to introduce you on a practical level to the topics being discussed. The names of those mentioned in the case studies have been changed.

This book was mainly written from the perspective of Susanne Matsudo-Kiliani, and Yukio Matsudo acted as co-writer and invaluably contributed his deep and extensive knowledge. We would like to thank David Brookes for his extraordinary help in proofreading and editing the English version of this book, which was originally written in German and then translated into English.

Susanne Matsudo-Kiliani and Yukio Matsudo

Chapter 1

The fascinating aspects of Nichiren Buddhism

> One of the meanings of "myō" is that we are already fully equipped. We are perfect just the way we are. Heaven is within us and we do not have to live in fear and worry.

Looking for a Buddhist practice

I had been looking for a Buddhist practice for quite a while. Buddhism had somehow accompanied me for the duration of my whole childhood. My grandfather had been passionately interested in it and set up a whole room full of books exclusively on Buddhism and Eastern philosophy. When he died, he left me some of his books and that's when I realized that Tiantai's book on the "Great Meditation" (Makashikan) was also among them.

I still remember sitting in his room reading books for hours and hours in this beautiful 200-year-old wooden Black Forest house. Whenever I did this, I just sank into another mysterious world that I was fascinated by.

My grandpa had experienced an extraordinary "out-of-body experience" during World War I. As a young medical doctor it was his task to look after the wounded soldiers and he had to march with his troop for days. At one point he was so completely exhausted after crossing a river that he collapsed. Suddenly, he saw himself hovering over his body, and perceived everything around him very precisely. He saw and heard everything his comrades were doing and saying, even though he was actually "unconscious" and outside of his body. He survived this incident and came "back into his body" again. But this experience had profoundly changed his understanding of life and it was something that he could never forget. He realized that he was not his body. He only inhabited his body. For a short wonderful time, he had experienced pure consciousness. Back in his day he could not find an opportunity to actually practice Buddhism, but from that day forward he was fascinated by the Buddhist concept that consciousness lives on after physical death. Thus, he read every single book that he could get about Buddhist or Eastern philosophy.

Part of my family karma

My grandpa knew how hard life can be. As a young child he lost both parents, who had died two years apart from each other. Afterwards he grew up with a very strict uncle who tried to discipline him. Very often he felt abandoned and homeless. My parents also died two years apart from each other.

Over the years, I discovered another similar karmic pattern between my grandfather and me. He also had a brother with whom he had completely fallen out with. Until today, nobody really knows what happened between the two of them. My grandfather's brother tried to visit my grandfather shortly before his death, when he was already very old. But my grandpa refused to see him. Whatever happened between them, it must have been something that my grandpa could not forgive until the end of his life.

Whenever I chanted, I felt more and more deeply that this energetic pattern was probably also stored in my subconscious. It actively showed itself in my life in the relationship with my own brother, who had always tried to destroy me out of extreme jealousy in any way you could think of. In deepening my daimoku practice, I gradually realized that I could not change him, but that I could surely change the way that I handled the situation. It was on me to decide in what way he could influence my life. I wondered if the cause of this terrible experience was to be found in my current existence or whether this pattern energetically originated in some earlier experiences of my ancestors.

I really started thinking about this, because I happened to discover the same surprising patterns of our family karma when I visited that part of my family that had migrated to the US more than three generations ago. Had all these information patterns been transferred to me as well?

Did you inherit your grandma´s emotions?

After all, this is what recent studies in the field of epigenetics suggest. They have provided evidence that memories of fear, for instance, are one of many things our ancestors pass down to us through our DNA. According to new insights of behavioral epigenetics, traumatic experiences such as violence or poverty in our ancestor's past leave molecular scars adhering to our DNA. This is often the case in the subsequent generations in negative life settings. Negative emotions such as grief, pain, unsuccessfulness or seemingly groundless feelings of guilt are prominent. Our own experiences and those of our parents and grandparents have never gone. Psychological and behavioral tendencies are inherited. That means you might not have just inherited your grandmother´s looks, but also her attitude towards men or her predisposition towards anxiety caused by the shortages that she suffered during World War II.

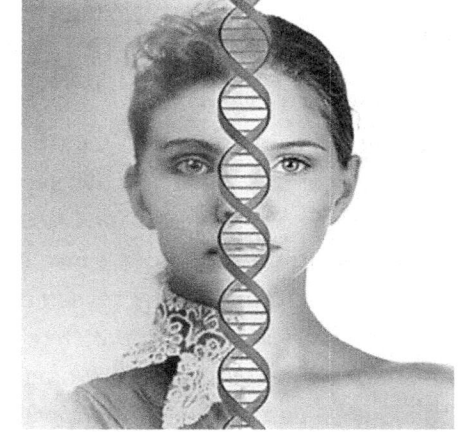

We are not at the mercy of our genes

In order to live a happy life, it is therefore necessary to recognize, clean and transform the karmic informational patterns of our ancestors.

Throughout the past, I became increasingly aware that this is exactly what the strong vibration of the cosmic energy of the **daimoku** causes to happen. I realized that I could transform those karmic patterns by transforming my own feelings of fear, anger and resentment. The less resentment that I felt towards those people who had hurt me, for instance, the less that I was stuck in those karmic patterns. Then these karmic patterns did not have any power over me and did not control me anymore.

For we are not at the mercy of our genes. The American biologist Bruce Lipton claims that it is our thoughts and emotions that determine which genes we switch on and off. It is not the genes themselves that determine whether or not we get the diseases that prevail in our family. It is the constantly recurring negative feelings that always switch these genes on that make us sick. However, experts also found out that positive emotions and laughter actually turn on the genes that keep us healthy.

It is our own feelings that have a decisive influence on how healthy or sick we are. In this sense, the dissolution and the transformation of one's own karma could therefore be described as being able to transform one's own thoughts and feelings.

Twin studies have recently revealed just how much your own consciousness is involved in the state of your health. There was the case of the two 90-year-old women who were identical twins with identical genes. One of them was really healthy and active, whereas the other one had become a case for nursing care and had developed a strong form of dementia. The healthy twin sister described her sick sister as always having been constantly worried and easily being upset about everything in her life.

> It is not the genes alone that determine how healthy or how ill you are. It is crucial to be able to interrupt your painful emotions, thoughts, and attitudes and transform them into positive, happy, and fulfilling emotions and attitudes.

Is life just happening to you?

But what exactly was my individual consciousness and in which way did it contain the experiences of my grandparents and my parents? When my parents died, I suddenly had no "home" to go to anymore. I felt that their death had a deep meaning for my life that went beyond my own personal pain. For the first time in my life I had completely lost my support system and in the end this made me realize that I had to open up to something greater than myself. Only then did I really begin to look for some Buddhist practice. Without this happening to me, I would not have been looking for a spiritual practice at such an early stage in my life.

At first I met the meditative practice of Tibetan Buddhism, which for a long time served to be a kind of an oasis for me, in order to forget the harsh and cold reality around me. I meditated a lot and found it very consoling to temporarily withdraw from this world in order to find peace within myself. But I was not really satisfied with my life. At that time, I did not realize that it was my own inner stories that I was constantly telling myself, my own thoughts, feelings, and attitudes that shaped my reality.

At the time, as I see it today, I was often focusing my thoughts on loss and separation, which often made me feel terrible. I thought that others had a home to go to and I didn´t. I thought more about the things that I didn't have in my life than about the things that I did have. I always thought that I was at a disadvantage. As long as I felt that way, however, then that would be the reality that I experienced. At the time, I didn't know that I had to change my beliefs in order to change my reality. I often asked myself: why does this happen to me? These thoughts made me feel lonely and depressed.

I wasn´t aware that my projected thoughts and feelings affected my energy. When I was sending out low-frequency, unhappy energy, I received low-frequency energy and experiences in return. I often felt a victim to my circumstances. I did not understand the connection between my inner mind-set and my outer circumstances. I thought that all these things making me sad and angry were just happening to me and I couldn't do anything about it. Little did I know, for I was soon to find out that life was not just something happening *to* me, it was happening *because of* me and even *through* me. It took me a while to understand that.

My encounter with Nichiren Buddhism

I had always dreamed about living in Spain for a while. Shortly after finishing my university studies in Germany, I succeeded in enrolling on a complementary study program supported by the European Union and took a 6-month foreign study course at a university in Madrid, Spain. I spent a wonderful time in this magnificent city, going to university and attending flamenco courses at one of the most renowned flamenco schools in the world, the Amor de Dios. That´s where I met a woman from Israel and we became very close friends. We were really enjoying our time in Madrid together. The whole time I was staying with a Spanish family, which improved my Spanish a lot. I really enjoyed it and came back to Germany after finishing my course at university.

That was in winter 1997 and it was really cold. I remember that unlike the warm and friendly nature of the people in Spain, I felt that the atmosphere in Germany was terrifyingly factual and cold.

I also had to look for a new apartment and get a job. I really wanted to stay in Spain, because I just felt comfortable there, but something deep inside me told me that I had to return to Germany because there was something waiting for me there.

Today I know that it was the right thing to do to listen to my intuition. Back in Germany, I temporarily moved in with a female friend and I realized that I hated to be dependent on someone else. I had always been very independent. Deep down I felt that I had to drastically change my situation.

One night I felt somehow discouraged and just wanted to forget everything. That´s why I went to the concert of an American friend of mine named Billy whose music I really liked. It was a mixture of blues, folk and country music. After the concert, we talked for a while. He told me that he was a Buddhist and chanted a certain mantra in front of a mandala, called the Gohonzon. He also described that while chanting he set himself concrete goals in order to realize them. That was completely new to me.

Being enchanted while chanting

Billy invited me to get to know his practice and I agreed. A few days later, I chanted daimoku for the first time in front of a Gohonzon at Billy's home. I still remember how I was drawn to this mandala. This specific, incredibly strong energy rising in my whole body was a completely different kind of energy from what I had known so far, and yet it immediately felt familiar to me. I was one with everything, feeling easy, blissful and full of joy. It felt like coming home. This has not changed to this day. From somewhere deep down fragments of memories came up, as if I had often chanted in front of this kind of mandala before. The energy stayed with me even after I finished chanting.

At the time, I regarded this Buddhist practice to be another form of meditation. However, I was really fascinated when Billy told me that you could actually change your concrete circumstances in life with this practice.

Could that really be true?

Did this mean I could chant for a job or an apartment? That sounded unbelievable. One day Billy introduced me to a woman who had a very intense way of chanting. She invited me to chant together with her. Not long before that she had suffered from multiple sclerosis but had managed to stop this disease by chanting **daimoku**.

She used to have almost unbelievable experiences as far as her health was concerned. As a nurse she had been infected with hepatitis C by a patient.

I watched her chanting intensively for several hours a day for a while and afterwards her blood check showed no trace of hepatitis C any more.

I liked this woman. She absolutely relied on the practice of **daimoku**. For her, the only important thing was the Gohonzon. She sometimes had rather chaotic circumstances in her life. When she told me about her difficult childhood, however, I started to understand why that was the case. But she always managed to "chant herself out" of her problems.

At one of the larger meetings I met another woman who had suffered from cervical cancer. Being a single mother with two children she just could not afford to die, she told me. Therefore she sat down in front of the Gohonzon and chanted almost uninterrupted for twelve hours. In the following week she visited her doctor, who told her that her cancer was completely gone and that he did not have any explanation at all for it.

The more such experiences I heard, the more curious I became. Could I really influence my physical condition and create situations in life that I could chant for? I really wanted to know and try myself.

Chanting to realize specific wishes

When I started chanting, I really appreciated that there was something that I could do in a very concrete way in order to improve the way that I felt. My mind became clearer and I began to feel much better about myself. Until then I thought that I simply could not change the way that I felt. Now I began to feel more motivated, and this new kind of hope encouraged me to look for a new job opportunity.

Fortunately there were no major health challenges that I had to face in my life, but I wanted to improve my career prospects. I provided my consciousness with some new ideas about what I wanted my life to be like. I wanted some clear and significant proof that my practice could work. I visualized myself earning three times as much per month, on a regular basis, because I wanted to move into a new apartment and I needed a new car. That was a lot more than I was used to, but I wanted a clear result.

I was tired of getting translation work at irregular intervals. Moreover, I really needed to rebuild my business contacts in Germany after coming back from Spain. This was a bit tedious at first, and sometimes I got an incredible amount of orders all at once, and at other times I did not have any income for weeks. I enjoyed translating and teaching English, but now I wanted to earn a specific, regular monthly sum. Therefore, I began to apply for new positions and assignments at all kinds of institutions, but I received one job rejection after another.

Every time that I was turned down, I felt almost paralyzed with panic. At that time I noticed that I often felt some anxiety and insecurity during the phases when I did not chant. I thought to myself: "Strange, since I've started chanting, I am having real anxiety attacks."

When I asked people for advice, the most common answer was: "Just keep chanting!" This kind of answer didn't satisfy me, however, because I really wanted to understand what was happening.

I didn't know it yet, but due to the chanting I must have had access to that part of my brain or consciousness where old, repressed feelings were stored. The whole thing could be described as a kind of cleaning-out process of my body and my mind.

Chanting daimoku dissolves old blockages

Today I know: You cannot activate your enlightened potential without shining the light into those dark places of your life. Just chanting for something and trying to realize your goals but pretending the dark places are not there is not going to work.

It was those layers of my subconscious mind that were blocking my connection to my enlightened consciousness and preventing me from fulfilling my wishes.

This situation can be explained with an example of dirt at the bottom of a glass. Just fill the glass with water and put it on a burner in order to heat it up. When the water starts circulating it starts to bring up the dirt from the bottom up to the surface. The power of daimoku sets a similar process in motion. The same thing happens when you start to detoxify your body. If something comes up that makes you feel bad it just means that all the toxins stored in your body will be released. Afterwards you will feel much better than before. If we don't detoxify, however, you might get sick.

Chanting daimoku can sometimes cause a series of detoxification responses on the emotional, physical and spiritual levels of your life.

Transform your own negativity

For the first time in my life, I became aware that I needed to transform my own inner negativity if I wanted to see changes. I felt that I had been confronted with fear and a sense of lacking all my life, and that this was exactly what I was supposed to overcome.

However, my ego was controlling me, since this feeling often prevented cosmic life energy from flowing through me and unfolding itself in my life. I noticed that the old stored energy was released by chanting. For many years, during my studies and the illness of my parents, I had always pulled myself together and suppressed my emotions. Even when I was very sad, I just had to grit my teeth in order to be able to work.

This way I managed to have the time to take my examinations in between those phases when I wasn´t working. After a while I had internalized the feeling that I had to do everything by myself. This had been part of my belief system all my life without me realizing it.

I had not become aware yet that it was precisely this unconscious conviction that repeatedly manifested itself in external reality. It was only when I replaced this belief with the new belief that I was always protected during chanting that my experienced reality changed.

The mystic coincidence of synchronicity

By now I had become acquainted with the teaching and practice of Nichiren Buddhism and was fascinated by the possibility of changing my reality through my own vision when I was chanting. First I really wanted to change my income situation. For two or three months, there was no sign that anything was changing on the outside. I applied again and again and felt that I really had to manage to achieve things this way. When I was chanting, I repeatedly visualized that I was earning a specific income and I deeply trusted the process that I was setting in motion.

Then one day in a supermarket I happened to meet an old fellow student of mine who I had not seen for many years after graduating from university. We started talking to each other and she told me that she was working as an editor for a very renowned publisher house, the German "Klett-Verlag" (Klett Publishing House). It turned out that they had a vacant position and were urgently looking for another editor for correcting the English-German entries of the latest edition of the Pons dictionary English-German. She gave me all the contact details and I quickly applied for that job.

There were some hurdles to overcome, though. The editor wanted me to make a sample translation that was quite challenging. I absolutely wanted to have this job, though, and I agreed to do it.

It was a very hot summer and I was living in a room right under the roof. It was very hot and sticky in my room as I worked on the translation. But I knew I wanted this job no matter what it would take, so I worked for two weeks from morning until night.

After having submitted the sample translation, the Chief Editor was very enthusiastic about my work and said that she really would like to give me the job, but she could only do this one year from now because of the company's budget plan. Since I desperately needed a job as soon as possible, I told her decisively that I would only be available to do the work at that very moment. I was quite surprised at myself, but I was so firmly decided to change my situation that I simply set up that condition. Since the Editor was really enthusiastic about my sample translation, she offered me the position right away. The best thing was that I could do the corrections of the dictionary entries comfortably at home and send her the results on a computer disk. Finally I had managed to have a regular monthly income of almost double the amount I had earned on a monthly basis so far. This alone could have well been considered a very good income.

However, my vision consisted of an even bigger income. This time I learned another important lesson: the answer of cosmic consciousness does not come as expected. The way things happen is always a surprise. I had expected that my old "strategy" would work when I applied directly to institutions I had previously worked for. I did all this at the time. But the solution came unexpectedly.

> My intention was supported by cosmic consciousness (**Nam-myō-hō-ren-ge-kyō**) and I was in the right place at the right time, without having planned it beforehand.

The event will find you

The same thing happened to me again in the same supermarket as before. "By coincidence" I met one of my former students whom a couple of years before I had been training to become a foreign language secretary. She was now working for a company near to where I lived and asked me whether I was still teaching English, because the company she was working for was looking for someone to teach business English to its employees.

This was exactly what I had been chanting for. I immediately contacted the person in charge. He told me to call him back another time. This happened again and again. After a while he admitted to me that he had wanted to see whether I was really interested in the job and whether I would actually call him back. He agreed to take me on. Everything seemed to look great until the process was suddenly stopped by the company's finance office who said that they could not take me on directly, since this kind of job would normally not be paid directly by them but by the personnel department of their parent company. By this time, however, I had already learned that such a firm "No!" on the outside was a challenge to deepen my faith and intensify my intention while chanting. Thus, I chanted very intensely to strengthen the image within me that I already had this job.

I just did not want to be unsettled by the external situation. It was not easy and took me a lot of courage to call the company's Financial Manager. But then something strange happened. During the phone call he decided that in my case the company would make an exception and hire me directly and pay for my job.

I could hardly believe it: together with my income I received from proofreading the dictionary corrections I had managed to triple my monthly income. I had manifested the exact amount of income that I had chanted for. On top of that, I had learned an important lesson: in order to really get ahead, I had to go beyond the boundaries of my present circumstances. In short:

> I was challenged to stop my old habits of thinking and feeling the same way over and over again.

I was deeply surprised that I had not achieved all this by my usual way of doing things. The event had just found me. The intention that I was holding while I was chanting had come true without much effort on my part. In a way, it had just come to me. It turned out that I was in the right place at the right time and that "by coincidence" I met the right people in a supermarket, who presented me with the opportunities that I had been waiting for. That was real synchronicity. Moreover, this time other people had really helped me, too.

I felt that it was the energy of **daimoku** that had activated a higher force to support me. Usually I had always done everything by myself by using my own personal willpower and effort. But I myself could have not arranged such a "coincidence", which was really mystic in nature. There was a higher intelligence at work that knew much more than I did. I was experiencing something well beyond my imagination and all I had to do was make it welcome. I realized that this is how you feel when you are in the flow and things run smoothly.

> You have to really take action and make the best out of such an opportunity. From that moment on it depends on your own effort to realize your wishes and goals.

Now I was really challenged to act in a very decisive way. This process required me to get out of my comfort zone. At this point, I was also asked to overcome many fears and tendencies within myself that might have prevented me from taking this opportunity.

> But the event itself had found me.

Chapter 2

Facing your blockages

Becoming aware of your emotional blockages

I was excited when I realized that it was possible to manifest my wishes by chanting **daimoku**. However, I also noticed very quickly that there was something that could delay or block the manifestation of my wishes. The more frequently that I chanted, the more intensely I became aware of the feeling of fear rising within me. This feeling was familiar to me from the time before I started chanting. I instinctively knew that I had to release this feeling that was blocking me from being who I really was. Every time that I began to chant, the feeling disappeared again quickly. Later on I became more and more conscious of the fact that it often controlled my inner condition.

I had experienced very early in life that things can easily and quickly fall apart on the outside. Especially when my mother was dying of breast cancer I felt a deep shock and pain inside of me. I quite vividly remember the feeling as if somebody had taken a knife and stabbed it right into my gut. I remember thinking: I wish there was *something* I could do to help her or to release my pain. At that time, however, there wasn´t anything that I could do, because I did not know about the possibility of chanting in front of a Gohonzon yet. It was only when I started chanting that I realized how much that experience had caused a constant feeling of fear and anxiety within me.

That was the first time that I became aware of my true inner feelings. Until then I had just locked my feelings up, hiding them even to myself. That was a phenomenon Nichiren had described very precisely. He was quite aware of our human tendency to get accustomed to feelings or situations that are not good for us.

> Insects that live on smartweed forget how bitter it tastes; those who stay long in privies forget how foul the smell is.
> *On Establishing the Correct Teaching for the Peace of the Land (1260)*

That is to say: You can get accustomed to everything after a while and start to consider your present situation as "normal". You may only notice that this is not the case when you get to know something completely different.

Using the example of Nichiren, when you are sitting on a toilet, you will get used to the stink. You will notice the bad smell only when you go out and get some fresh and clean air. After having smelled fresh air, though, you can't stand the old smell anymore. This basically means that only when you become aware in what way your present situation is not good for you, will you start to change it. That's why it is so essential to increase the fresh energy of **daimoku**.

Exercise 1: You can't stand it any more

Have you ever had a similar experience to what Nichiren described?

What was it that you couldn't put up with any more, i.e. a certain situation/person/behavior/object after you started chanting?

Becoming true to yourself

I became more aware of my specific pattern of thinking and feeling. I became much truer to myself. I realized that deep down most of my actions were driven by the constant nagging feeling of some kind of fear. I pumped myself and all of my friends up with tons of food supplements and vitamins, because deep down I was in constant fear that someone I love could become ill and die again.

I had the constant nagging fear that someone could try to make me feel outcast and unloved again, the way my brother had always tried to harm me. I feared having no support and no protection. But I also realized that it wasn´t just me clinging to that feeling. Suddenly I sensed that almost everybody around me was holding on to fear in one or many areas of their life.

Different strategies to cope with fear

The same might also apply to you. Maybe you are fearful of not having enough money or maybe you are afraid of being left alone. Maybe you are afraid of having no pension once you are old. Maybe you are afraid of getting cancer. Maybe you are afraid of not being smart enough or not having enough. In my case, it was almost all of these things. I lived in a constant state of anxiety and I did not even realize it.

For many years, I did everything to anesthetize my fear with "being busy", numbing myself with a lot of activities and working too much. I worked so hard that there was no room for worrying about things or for dealing with my fear. The funniest thing was, I was not even *aware* of it.

Exercise 2: Are you worried?

What are you worried about or afraid of?

What is your specific strategy to cope with your worry or fear apart from chanting?

Fear was present every time I thought about work coming in. It was there every time I was looking at my bank account. It was there every time I fell out with a friend. It was there every Christmas, because that's when I most painfully felt the absence of my family. It was there every time that I was too nice to people because I feared losing them.

This changed drastically the more I chanted to the Gohonzon. Chanting **daimoku**, I could not suppress all of this anymore. All of my suppressed fears came up with a strong energetic surge. I suddenly opened my mind to my fear-based patterns. I realized that I had a lot of fear-based beliefs from my past that I kept projecting onto my internal movie screen that soon would become the film of my future, if I did not change the script.

Exercise 3: Are you projecting your past?

What fear-based stories from the past are you projecting onto your present life?

How are these stories blocking you from feeling happy and supported?

This or something better

I remember that I still reacted with a lot of panic whenever I chanted for something and it did not turn out the way that I wished it to. Once I chanted for a part-time teaching job at a language institute and I did not get it. I remember sitting in my kitchen in panic, asking myself why this had not worked out. I took a leap of faith and continued chanting. A few days later I got a phone call from another institute I knew that offered me a similar job in the same region. This institute offered me much more money than I would have earned had I got the job that I had chanted for.

That's when I began to understand that there was a higher order behind all of this. I started to cultivate the soothing feeling that my intention was carried by universal life energy and was in the process of manifesting itself in its own time.

My job was to receive and welcome everything good that showed up in my reality and then do my best at it. It was important to be specific and clear in what I wanted when I was chanting. However, there was something I really had to learn:

> I had to let go of the outcome.

I learned to stop constantly looking for proof or getting impatient when my intended result did not show up. I just had to trust that something better would show up. When you surrender to the Gohonzon and just trust, that's when you release energetic resistance. That's when you raise your vibration and open your heart to all possibilities.

I know that everybody can suddenly be affected by fear, though. Even after things have been going absolutely fantastically for a while, the feeling of fear can knock you down. Even if we are strongly committed to our practice, we can easily lose confidence when we feel powerless over a situation. You lose your job, you lose a loved one or get a terrible diagnosis. I realized that I was almost programmed to react to any situation of uncertainty with fear.

Since I have had the Gohonzon, however, I can handle the feeling of fear much better. I know deep down that I am always guided and supported by the power of **daimoku**, even if doesn't feel that way when I am depressed or anxious. But it no longer takes that long to transform that feeling. Fear doesn't keep me paralyzed or make me hide in the bedroom all day any more. Now I know that there is actually something *I can do*. I just have to make it to the Gohonzon and soon this invigorating energy rises from deep inside of me. This inner change is always reflected on the outside.

Exercise 4: The Gohonzon has your back

How would you feel if you knew that you were always being supported, protected and guided by a power that is bigger than your ego (even if it doesn't look that way)?

The Gohonzon made it possible for me to connect to this universal energy, my true self. Allowing this guiding and stabilizing flow of universal energy move through me, is what really stabilized me.

I started to feel a sense of certainty no matter what was going on in my life. Whenever I am aligned with this loving and invigorating presence, I feel genuinely confident and enthusiastic and people resonate with my energy.

When I am completely in sync with the frequency of the Gohonzon, I feel safe, full of energy, calm and in harmony with everything that is happening around me. Then the world and all its fear and lack and limitation can no longer affect me. I just trust. I know that I am protected and guided. When I am out of alignment with the power of this universal energy, I feel tired, stuck, left alone, unsupported, weak and angry. Fear is back again. That's when I start chanting immediately. I surrender my fear to the Gohonzon. By doing so, I do not feed this feeling any more. That's when the hopeful and positive feelings return. Today I clearly know the difference between what if feels like to be aligned to universal energy versus what it feels like when I am not. I can also tell the difference by how the outside world responds to my inner power.

> Throughout the day when you notice a fearful projection placed on your worldly experience, just say to yourself: I surrender this fear to the Gohonzon and let universal life energy take over.

To what extent do you see yourself as a victim?

In the course of my practice, I realized that I was blaming many external things for my not being satisfied with my life. I projected my own beliefs. Deep inside, I was convinced that life was hard and that I always had to fight alone for everything. This was my conditioning and perception.

I had not been aware of this mental mechanism, but now my hidden feelings and beliefs came to the surface. I was full of anger because I had the feeling that someone was always being preferred over me or that someone wanted to push me out. It all had to do with my brother, who had always tried to take away from me everything that was important to me. I still felt that no one would support me if I really needed it most. Those were the perceptions of the past.

But now I had access to the greatest power of the universe through the Gohonzon. My feelings of resentment and being at a disadvantage turned slowly into neutrality. Suddenly I felt more and more that another person's actions had no power to influence my life, my happiness, my prosperity, or my success in any way. That's something that I could only do to myself.

Exercise 5: Are you a victim?

Do you think that a certain person is responsible for your current situation or how you feel?

When chanting to the Gohonzon, can you feel the freedom that as long as you align yourself to the frequency of your Higher Self, no one else can determine your happiness or your destiny?

What is your victim story?

Through chanting I became aware of my victim story. When I realized my hidden thoughts and feelings was when it started to lose its power. I noticed that I often expressed my victim consciousness when I talked to people. "He did this to me. She did this to me. They said this about me. I did this wrong."

I felt as if my destiny was determined by something or someone outside of myself or by my perception of what somebody had done to me or said about me in the past.

Do you think that there is somebody or something to blame for your situation? Maybe it´s your astrological sign or your numbers. Maybe you are mad at your past employer or your past relationships. If only your partner behaved differently. At any rate, you might think, it´s definitely your parent´s fault. In this case, you are walking around subconsciously allowing that blame to rule your life. This can easily control you. Nonetheless, there is one big reason why it is so important to give up your victim story. It´s very easy.

You have to take your power back!

If you are afraid of being victimized, afraid of being taken advantage of, afraid of being disappointed, afraid of loss, then where is your attention going? The attention is going to your fear, into that particular victim story.

Where is your attention going?

You might often think, "I'm afraid that I'm never going to make it." As we shall see later in this book, your thought forms are energy that influences your outer reality.

If you place your attention on what you want, you might say to yourself, "I really want a greater way of living, I really want greater prosperity in my life." Or you could also say, "I really don´t want to be poor, I don't want to be unhealthy." As we pointed out before, the quantum field doesn't know the difference between what you want and what you don´t want. It only knows what you turn your attention to and what you are interested in.

This is how you put yourself into victim consciousness, by constantly identifying what you don´t want. This is very important because often when you ask people what they want in life, they give you a long list of what they don´t want. So where is their attention going? Their attention is going to what they don´t want. That´s why it is so important to give up your victim story. *Today* you can begin to release some of the energy around your victim story through the power of identifying it. There are certain statements you want to be aware of:

Exercise 6: Who is to blame?

Do you ever say things like, "Somebody else did this to me. It´s somebody else´s fault. It's the world's fault"?

Well, the story becomes reality, unless you give the story up. After I started chanting, I recognized the areas in my life where I was operating as a victim. At the same time I realized how many people around me were living as victims as well.

Gradually my perception started to change and I stopped seeing myself as always being at a disadvantage. I realized that as long as I was sending out the vibration of feeling *disadvantaged,* the experience of being *advantaged* could not find me, because it was not a vibrational match.

Nowadays I am much more aware of whenever I start to go into victim mode. That´s when I immediately visualize a Gohonzon in front of me and align to a higher frequency, in order to better my life. Over the years, I started to recognize my own qualities and realized that by focusing on what I don´t have in contrast to what other people have, I only radiate the frequency of "I am missing something". As long as I do this, I will, of course, "miss something". That´s when I understood why you should chant until "your heart is content", as they say. Whenever you reach that feeling while chanting, you radiate the information that all your needs are met regardless of your outer circumstances. That's the signal that usually starts to change your outer circumstances.

Therefore I started to focus on what I had instead of what I didn´t have. Whenever I did this, I radiated a frequency of deep gratefulness and things started to get better on the outside. Whenever I am grateful for what I have, I am not so much involved in conversations about victim consciousness.

Exercise 7: Overcoming your unwholesome story

Get honest with yourself. What is your favorite low-frequency story and how does it make it you feel?

Are you willing to give up that story?

_____

How would your life look without that story?

_____

While chanting, think to yourself: I am determined to reconnect to my true essence and power. I surrender this story to the Gohonzon and get out of the way to let cosmic consciousness find a solution.

_____

The old must make room for the new

I often observed a specific phenomenon in the lives of people who began practicing **daimoku** intensively. Everything old that energetically did not fit any more suddenly seemed to collapse. I also experienced this, too. When I began to practice, relationships that were not really good for me broke apart very quickly or changed.

I realized that ultimately something had changed within my own consciousness and that I perceived certain people completely differently than before. Somehow I had interrupted the energy flow of my old life and, focusing more on the Gohonzon, I withdrew my energy from the people and things that connected me to my past.

I realized that my outer life was reorganizing itself in order to match the visions that I had created while chanting. Often I experienced that things on the outside were stirred up in a very unexpected way, because I had invested a lot of energy to create something new. Now something new was emerging. Many familiar situations had to go in order to make space for the new to arrive. Each time I chanted a lot with other people, I felt that I was on a new way. Coming back home, however, I was always confronted with my past. That was the moment to continue chanting and to stay aligned to the frequency of my new future. I realized that I was changing.

This occurred to me especially in the relationship with one of my aunts whom I always visited for Christmas and Easter after my parents had died. However, we had a long family history with her. When my parents were still alive she used to hurt my mother a lot. The more I chanted, I saw this mean side of her more clearly. I became deeply aware that she had often damaged my parents' relationship and burdened our family life. My father, however, never had the courage to stand up to her, because she was his elder sister. Now I was no longer willing to excuse or tolerate her arrogant and often hurtful nature, for I simply saw her deep selfishness behind her behavior. I could no longer deny it.

On the other hand, I also began to feel sorry for her, because I now realized that she could not act in a different way, as she was trapped in her own state of life. Her behavior only led to more and more loneliness and frustration in her life. Suddenly I saw how she really felt.

It took me a long time to understand that our relationship had changed since the time that I'd begun to chant intensively. Something within me had changed and obviously my aunt could not deal with this change. I no longer fit into the picture that she'd had of me all those years.

Suddenly I was more self-assured and happier. In the beginning I did not understand why she was so allergic to this. But after a while I realized that every success I had and every progress I made caused her to feel even more dissatisfied with her own life. I remember when I was flying to Japan for the first time. She murmured that she had to wait until she was retired until she had been able to make such a long-distance flight. When I got married, she complained that there had been no men available when she was young, because they had all died in the Second World War. The happier I became, the less she could stand it.

I observed that this happens quite often. Other people in your old environment try to pull you down energetically when they realize that now you are vibrating on a different frequency. And we actually do have a different frequency when we chant daimoku, as we shall see later on.

Sometimes people in your environment feel threatened by this because it indirectly challenges them to change. Sometimes you become a mirror for their own frustration and their mental poisons. Some people will go away if they cannot keep pace with your change. Instead, new friendships are being made that better fit your new vibration.

With other people, however, I started to become milder when I suddenly realized that deep down they were acting out of fear or despair. That's when their behavior could not really hurt me anymore, because I suddenly felt a lot of compassion for them. I noticed how much my perception had changed.

> The changes in my state of life actually led to new experiences in my life. My energy had changed.

The chanting helped me to deal with my difficult states of mind: whenever I felt stressed, in a low mood, when I was distracted or upset. There was one thing that I felt very clearly. I could no longer avoid transforming my mental states of anxiety and anger, because now I knew how positive this clear energy of daimoku made me feel.

The practice of daimoku has helped me to create a new mind, thinking different thoughts and feeling different feelings. At the time I did not know it, but the practice of daimoku led to brain changes that helped me to feel more stable, secure and optimistic. My mind was changing. And so was my brain. But more about that later on.

Chapter 3
Consciousness is energy

> What you think, you become. — Buddha

Our thoughts are real forces

An old Buddhist principle tells us that you will become what you think. Therefore your karma is basically defined as the result of what you *think, speak* and what you *do*. According to recent research, most of us think about sixty thousand thoughts a day, 80% of which are negative. Research also shows that every thought has a clear consequence. In this case the so-called "law of resonance" can be applied to explain the phenomenon that the events you encounter in your life don't just happen by chance. They are attracted to you by what you are consciously or unconsciously thinking. There is a certain causality between your inner mindset and your experiences in the outer world. That´s why it is important to avoid saying "I can´t do it" just because you feel insecure or controlled by your own fear of failure. Such a negative expression concerning your self-image contradicts the power of daimoku that aligns your consciousness to the infinite cosmic consciousness.

Do you often think or say to yourself that you are fat, ugly or not good enough and that you will never be successful? Or do you think and say to yourself that you are amazing, worthy and beautiful? Words and thoughts are much more powerful than you can imagine. Try to be aware of which names and labels that you use to define yourself.

This can also make a difference in manifesting what you want, or what you don't want. Each word you speak possesses its own unique vibration that is felt inside your body the moment you say it. The same principle applies to the vibrational power of chanting daimoku. It´s a vibration you can feel in a physical sense. You may still remember the surprising results of Gas Discharge Visualization (GDV) measurement regarding our energy field and energy centers (chakras), as presented in our book *Change Your Energy – Change Your Life: Nichiren Buddhism 3.0*.

The intention of peace creates peace

Thoughts represent an energy that goes in all directions looking for a similar energy. When such a similar energy is met, there is some resonance. This phenomenon explains why like always attracts like or why thoughts actually become reality. Once we understand that our thoughts are real forces, we also understand why external situations are influenced by what we wish, visualize or try to achieve. Whatever we focus on within the invisible realm of our thoughts eventually manifests into outer form.

There was an interesting study about this initiated by the journalist and author Lynne McTaggart. She wanted to see whether the power of thought and the power of intention can actually influence a physical surrounding thousands of kilometers away. She set up an intention experiment with the Russian physicist Konstantin Korotkov, who invented the GDV-measurement device. We used this kind of measurement in order to measure the energy changes in our personal energy fields as well as the changes of the energy in the room while we were chanting daimoku. Lynne used the same device to find out about the effects of group intention.

Lynne had the following idea when she was taking part at the *World Happiness Summit* in Miami, USA earlier in 2017: She wanted to see if the intention of her audience of 1,000 people could in some way affect a bottle of water sitting in Dr. Korotkov´s office in St. Petersburg, Russia thousands of kilometers away. Would this be possible? Dr. Korotkov had set up certain equipment in order to measure the energetic changes in the room, all of it feeding into a computer system. In the following picture you can see the devices that were being used. Some of them can pick up changes in the electrical charge of a room due to their sensitivity to changes in environmental electromagnetic fields:

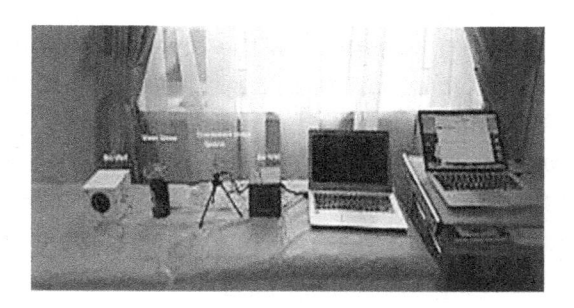

Source: http://theintentionexperiment.com/korotkov1

Sending love to water

The experiment was about to begin. Lynn's audience in Miami started to arouse the feeling of love within themselves and imagined sending it directly to the water over there. During this time, Dr. Korotkov had turned on his equipment in order to measure any changes in his office. After Lynne had texted him that the audience had finished, he turned off his devices. Then he started to analyze the measurements and sent Lynne the results a few hours later. Indeed, the intention of the audience had caused an amazing effect. There was a huge change in the electromagnetic charge in the entire room

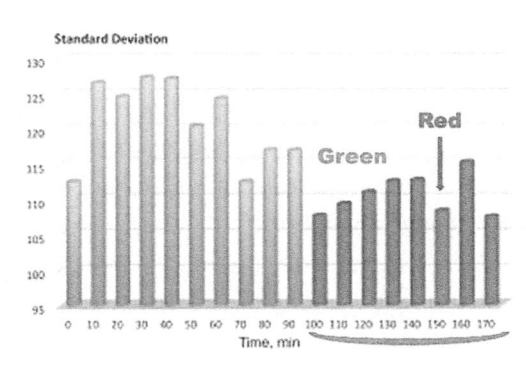

Source: http://lynnemctaggart.com/the-miami-korotkov-water-experiment/

housing the bottle of water. You can see the changes in the following chart.

The green bars show the time *before* the experiment started when Lynne was still talking to her audience and the red bar shows the time *during* the audience's intention, i.e. while one thousand Americans sent the intention of love to the bottle in Russia. The lowered position of the red bar represents a smaller signal which indicates essentially a calmer environment with less charge. Although some people may consider such an experiment to be not completely scientific in a strict sense, it does give some indication that we all have an enormous capacity to create calm and peace in our environment even thousands of kilometers away. That means we actually can have an influence on some hot spots on this Earth.

That's when I understood that there is a huge effect when hundreds of people chant for world peace during a Kōsenrufu gongyō, for instance. Kōsenrufu gongyō is a practice regularly carried out by the SGI (Sōka Gakkai International) that consists in citing parts of the Lotus Sutra (Gongyō) with the aim to contribute to worldwide peace. In such a ceremony, there is a directed intention of peace which is even amplified by chanting it directly to the Gohonzon.

The intention of love and peace actually creates
more calm and peace in your environment.

The feeling and intention of peace within you creates peace on the outside. As Lynne McTaggart puts it, "With all the terrorist activity on our doorsteps, a collective intention of peace could be our strongest weapon."

Many further experiments in consciousness research indicate that thought is a tangible energy that is infectious and can have a physical impact on events, and on living and non-living things. I myself have often observed that the positive thoughts and intentions we send while chanting act as a positive, infectious energy that shield us from negative intention.

The power of intention has no limit

Consciousness research suggests that your thoughts and your intention are a power that alters your surroundings, irrespective of time and space. That's an astonishing assertion of which I would have been very skeptical if I had not experienced this phenomenon myself. In April 2017, I took part in one of the intention experiments carried out by researcher and author Lynne McTaggart. The whole experiment involved around 70 people and took place via a web conference. After a while participants were divided into groups of two and we were connected with each other so that we could interact. My internet partner was a woman from the USA called Joanne. I started talking to her and found out certain personal aspects about her, i.e. that she had a dog and that she lived in Chicago and so on. I told her that I lived in Heidelberg, Germany and we were talking about the fact that thousands of kilometers were actually between us and we were living in completely different time zones.

After a while we were asked to prepare for the experiment. One of us would "send" the other an image of an object that had some emotional importance to the sender. The other person would be the "receiver" – in our case, I would be open to receiving Joanne's image.

Then the experiment started and I knew that Joanne was imagining an object that I was supposed to figure out. I focused myself on receiving what she was sending and the first image that came to my mind was a tree. This idea was very strong and I kept seeing a tree, but then suddenly I also "saw" the image of a beach and I "heard" the soothing sound of an ocean. A tree on a beach at the ocean? My analytical mind started interfering immediately and I thought that this image didn´t make sense. In the surroundings where I was brought up I hadn't associated a tree with a beach, rather with some mountains or hills. Suddenly I realized that there was some kind of noise on the line and I thought that this noise must have evoked the idea of an ocean in my mind. However, the strongest image I felt was that of a tree. Suddenly I had the same strong feeling I used to have at a certain spot in Mallorca, a Spanish island in the Mediterranean Sea, when my husband and I were sitting on a beach.

When the time was over, I was asked to reveal to Joanne what I had received and she was supposed to tell me what she had been sending. I told her that I actually did not just see one object but that I had the impression of a whole scene. I felt a tree on a beach and the sea behind it. I told her openly that this did not make any sense to me. However, she was very surprised and told me immediately, "But that is *exactly* what I was sending to you. I was thinking of a tree on a beach, which used to be a place I liked going to, but nowadays the tree doesn't exist anymore."

When she told me this I felt shivers running down my spine. Could that really be possible? Had I just completely sensed a picture somebody had "sent" to me thousands of kilometers away? I had often read that the power of intention transcends time and space, but was the power of intention *that* real? In my case, the power of intention had definitely transcended space. Joanne told me immediately that she had been looking at a picture of this tree while she was sending it and that she would send me the picture now via Facebook. I was very excited and waited to see the photograph that Joanne was sending to me.
And there it was: exactly the scene that I had sensed.

This little experiment made it absolutely real to me that the power of intention has no limit and goes beyond space and time. There were thousands of kilometers between Joanne and I, and we had never met or talked to each other before. Nevertheless, there was a connection between us and I could sense exactly the picture and the emotion that she was "sending" to me. That´s when I realized how powerful it is when you chant for someone.

> It does not matter where the person is you are sending your intention to.
> The power of your intention will reach the person, because we are all part of one big consciousness. We are all energetically connected.

Others know what you are feeling

This little experiment with Joanne made me realize on a very personal level that our thoughts are not exclusively located in our heads. We are constantly leaking our thoughts and ideas and forming psychic internet connections all the times. Our thoughts and emotions are a real, tangible force. Many more experiments like this have made it clear to me that we are each very much like an open channel and that others pick up the emotional charge of what we are thinking. Whatever you are thinking or feeling about a certain person is not just in your head or your heart. The other person feels it clearly on an invisible level and reacts accordingly to it. That´s why other people change once we change our attitude towards them.

You may imagine yourself to be a powerful radio tower that is constantly broadcasting your thoughts and feelings. Every thought and feeling that you have is answered in a synchronous way as though you have made a request. In this way, you are forming your own life with your own thoughts and getting a response that matches your broadcast. Therefore there is no need to wonder why certain things are happening to you. The first step to break this causality chain is to become aware of what you are thinking most of the time, even what you are "thinking" unconsciously. Therefore it is very important to check upon the thoughts and feelings you are sending out.

Exercise 8: Are you judging others?

What do you think about other people?

_____

Become aware when you are judging someone in any way.
Try to change that thought into a positive one or send **daimoku** to that person in order to improve their state of life and to improve your relationship with that person.

_____

What is your main negative thought? Do you often think:

Why is this happening to me? _____

I just don´t have enough. _____

Nobody loves me. _____

Things are getting worse. _____

I am alone and can´t do this. _____

How could you replace these thoughts with a positive alternative?

_____

What could you be thinking instead?

_____

Write down your negative thoughts and turn them into a positive outlook.

Thought forms are tangible energy

Any intensive thought that you bear, be it positive or negative, will sooner or later affect your life. Just to give you an example: I had a realization one sunny day in Autumn 2016. I was in my car ready to go into town. The car just would not start. As it turned out, the engine had fully broken without any prior indication. All of this happened at a moment when I least needed it and it really made me feel frustrated. I started to feel like a victim of circumstance.

For years this nice car had been my dream come true, to drive a sporty convertible, and finally I had been able to afford it. But lately I had been more and more internally complaining about it, because it was too small to transport things or give somebody else a lift. Every year I dreaded that it would snow in winter because the car often got stuck in snow. I was even regularly talking to my husband about how we needed a "winter-proof car". And now the engine of this expensive, wonderful car was just gone. The garage told us they could not repair it. Unexpectedly we needed to buy a new car.

This incident taught me that you have to be careful *what* you ask for and *how* you ask for the outcome of what you want. If you don't do it with a positive, grateful and expectant intention, you might not like the way your intention shows up in reality. The situation reflected my inner attitude. Somehow, I had even *created* it. This incident really made me become aware of my unconscious intentions, which perhaps manifest even more often than our conscious ones. In this case I had the feeling that it was my complaining about my wonderful car that suddenly made it disappear from my life.

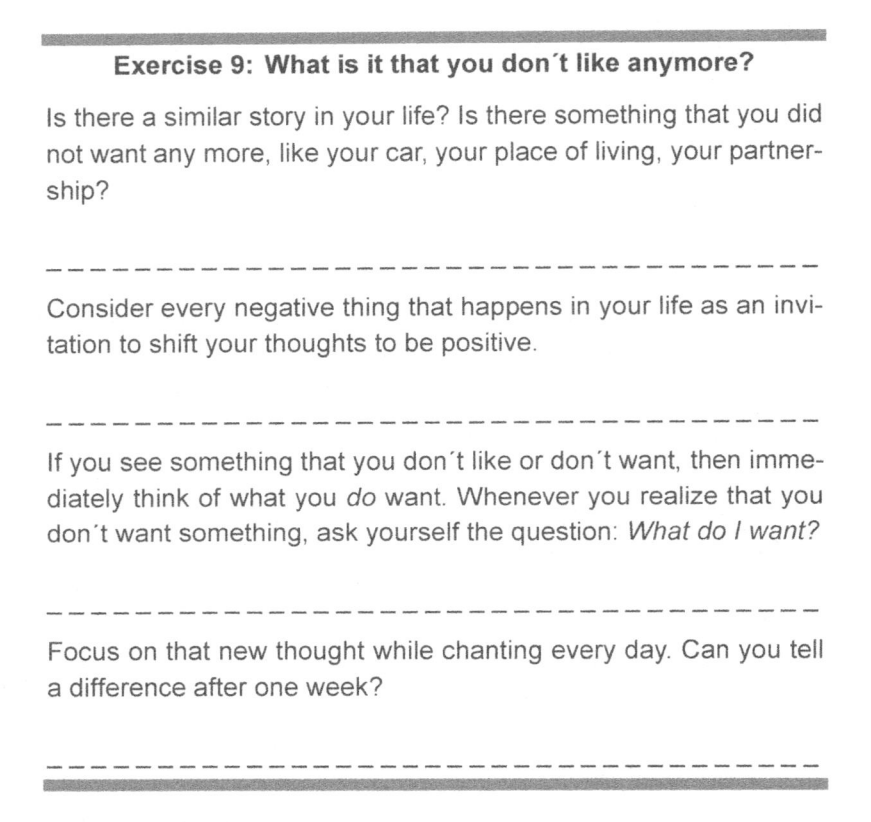

> **Exercise 9: What is it that you don't like anymore?**
>
> Is there a similar story in your life? Is there something that you did not want any more, like your car, your place of living, your partnership?
>
> --
>
> Consider every negative thing that happens in your life as an invitation to shift your thoughts to be positive.
>
> --
>
> If you see something that you don't like or don't want, then immediately think of what you *do* want. Whenever you realize that you don't want something, ask yourself the question: *What do I want?*
>
> --
>
> Focus on that new thought while chanting every day. Can you tell a difference after one week?
>
> --

Your negative intention may become reality

Bestselling author Lynne McTaggart suggests that every thought, just as our hopes, desires and longings, has an independent energy that changes the molecular structure of our environment. Everything depends on our thought energy. If things do not work out the way that you would like them to be, ask yourself whether your thoughts lack clarity and force.

We need to be constantly aware of what we are thinking. What we are thinking becomes reality. First our internal reality and then, after a period of time, our outer reality. Without this kind of awareness, we just feel, think and act on autopilot. If we do not want to experience our negativity on the outside, we definitely need a renewal of our minds.

I further realized the power of thought energy when I talked to a woman who had already been practicing for a couple of years. Sometimes she took the chanting seriously and that's when she progressed and managed to get a better apartment, for instance. But most of the time she fell back into her old patterns of pessimistic thinking. That's when she did not chant seriously. She was a teacher for handicapped children and she kept telling everybody that she was fed up with her job. She really wanted to do something else but she could not see any way out. That's why she often used to say, "I wish I'd be ill, so at least I wouldn't have to work anymore." My husband Yukio advised her that she should be very careful not to think or talk like this, because if she continued this way she might eventually become ill. She did not take his advice very seriously and continued in her own way. Three years later her wish to become ill became true and she needed a heart operation. Now she was too weak to go to work again. She had reached her "goal" and could become an early pensioner. When I visited her in hospital, she told me that she really regretted not having appreciated being healthy before, because now she did not have the energy to really enjoy life. At the time I was actually quite shocked by how accurately her "wish" had become reality. She had unconsciously "intended" to become ill.

Think of thoughts as flowers or weeds in a garden. Try to pull out weak, negative thoughts (weeds) by inviting stronger, more powerful thoughts to grow (flowers). Focus on them more often. This is easier said than done, if it is true that 80% of our thoughts tend to be negative, as researchers are telling us. This is where the vibrating power of *daimoku* comes in, which interrupts that vicious circle in a very concrete way, as we shall see in the following chapters.

> ### Exercise 10: Focus on your thoughts
>
> What are your predominant thoughts concerning your health, your relationships, your career and your money situation?
>
> _____
>
> Do you appreciate your partner, your job or your money situation? Would you like your thoughts to become reality?
>
> _____
>
> Are you creating positive thoughts and for how long do you keep them in your consciousness?
>
> _____
>
> Are you falling back to negative thinking after a short period of time?
>
> _____
>
> Try to keep positive thoughts in your mind for as long as possible.

The Gohonzon as an amplifier of our thoughts and feelings

The German physicist Fritz-Albert Popp discovered that all living things radiate tiny currents of light, tiny codes of light emissions. He called them "biophoton emissions". Moreover, he discovered that we're not only sending them, but we're also receiving them from our environment. We're communicating with our environment every moment. What this insight suggests is that we're a little like a television set and a television broadcasting station both at the same time.

Likewise, with intention—which is just another kind of energy—you are sending and receiving at every moment. Your messages are being heard and replied to on a quantum level all day and all night long. It's not just that half-hour when you are chanting in the morning and when you have a power thought, but all the other 23 and a half hours of your day. All those purposeful aims that you have, all those judgments you hold about people, all of your secret prejudices, every last mendacious thought, that all becomes your life's intention too. That becomes the thing that you're sending, whether you know it or not.

Chanting daimoku may therefore be understood as a specific action to send a message in terms of a thought, an intention or even an image. When we are chanting daimoku to the Gohonzon in a very focused way, our thoughts and feelings are simultaneously answered by our environment. The Gohonzon acts as an "amplifier" of our intentions, which at the same time possesses the power of transformation.

Whatever we send out is reflected with the same energetic strength on the stage of our lives. However, this amplifier also has its own energy signature when we chant: namely, the energy of the highest enlightened state of consciousness.

Since thoughts and feelings have their own energetic frequency, we feel more intensively the thoughts and feelings that do not fit into this highest state of life. I realized that the more we practice daimoku, the more that negative thoughts become so intolerable to us that we are forced to replace them with positive thoughts and higher-vibrating feelings.

Become crystal clear about what you want

Whenever I used to think about my thoughts, wishes and intentions, I had the impression that they were exclusively in my head, so to say. But the latest research suggests that any intention is an energy that has a physical shape and is as real as the chair on which we are sitting. Lynne McTaggart found out in her experiments that intention has a "rebound effect". What we send out comes back to us.

To those who study Nichiren Buddhism, it is clear that this is something that Nichiren knew almost 750 years ago. Nichiren reassures us that the vision and the intention we have when we are chanting is something real that we will definitely experience in reality. In this context he writes:

> The prayers offered by a practitioner of the Lotus Sutra will be answered just as an echo answers a sound, as a shadow follows a form, as the reflection of the moon appears in clear water, as a mirror collects dewdrops, as a magnet attracts iron, as amber attracts particles of dust, or as a clear mirror reflects the color of an object. *On Prayer (1272)*

Nichiren made it quite clear that the result of what you manifest in life will be exactly like the prayer or the intention that you put out.

This means you need a very clear, precise and strong vision of what you want. If you just have a vague idea or if your intention lacks power then the result in your life will be like a weak echo that follows a weak sound. When your scattered, busy mind can hold its focus in a single direction, you have taken the first step to initiate a new result in your life.

Thoughts and intentions are a physical thing – a tangible energy that has the amazing power to influence your world.

Can you measure your state of mind?

This "thing" can be measured. How does this work? Quite simply, our brain is electrochemical in nature and its electrical activities in the form of brainwaves can be measured, which reveals some of our thoughts and feelings. When the neurons in our brain are activated and fire together, they generate electromagnetic fields that can be measured by an EEG brain scan.

This was very fascinating to us and we wanted to learn more about it. If the aim of chanting *daimoku* is to gain access to an expanded state of consciousness, then we must, of course, know how to get there. Was the key to this altered state of consciousness to be found in changing our brainwaves?

Chapter 4
Can we measure the transformation?

Can you measure the effects of daimoku?

How can you actually explain why millions of people have had surprising experiences chanting daimoku in order to overcome difficult situations in their life, or in order to fulfill their wishes and even to heal their diseases? In the previous chapter we quoted Nichiren who said, "No prayer of a daimoku practitioner will remain unanswered just as a magnet attracts iron." In order to explain this mechanism, we pointed out how important your thoughts and intensions are, independent of whether you are aware of them or not. As we shall see, any thought and any intention has some concrete effect.

Therefore, we really wanted to know what exactly happens when we chant daimoku. In our book *Nichiren Buddhism 3.0* we presented the results of measuring the energetic state of our body while chanting. We found out that you can considerably raise your energy even chanting for only ten minutes. Furthermore, we realized that there were significant changes in our energy centers. This change of energy can explain the effects of daimoku and makes it understandable why chanting daimoku improves your physical energy, your health and therefore your overall well-being.

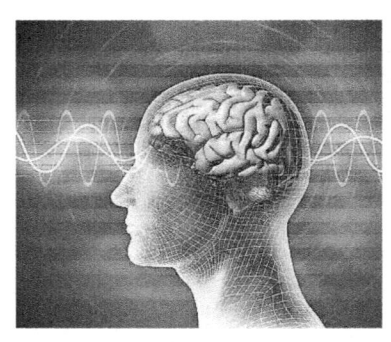

Your brain produces waves

Neuroscientists have found out that every thought and every activity in our brain produces some electrical frequency. We were asking ourselves whether there were measurable changes in our brainwaves when we are chanting and what condition we had to reach in order to really change our reality.

Our first measurement attempts

There have already been a great number of experiments that measure the changes of brainwaves during various forms of silent meditation. However, we didn't know whether we could really measure anything at all when we chant daimoku with our eyes open. That's why we turned to a well-established neuroscientific research institute in Germany that had developed a method using sound frequencies in order to improve learning difficulties and health problems caused by stress. The institute already had some experience in measuring the brainwaves of people during various forms of meditation.

We therefore asked the institute if it was possible to measure our own brain frequencies while we are chanting daimoku. The assistant in charge didn't know anything about the practice of daimoku, she made an offer to do so if we were ready to measure the effect of the institute's method using sound frequencies beforehand. She told me that afterwards I could chant for ten minutes and she would then also measure my brain frequencies while I was doing so. In this case the measurement during the chanting was regarded as a first trial to check whether it was possible to measure anything at all. If the first measurement was successful, a more elaborate measurement could possibly follow.

Before the measurement could take place, four points were determined on my head at which the brain frequencies were measured. The institute had developed its own data processing system for measuring brainwaves and for presenting the subsequent

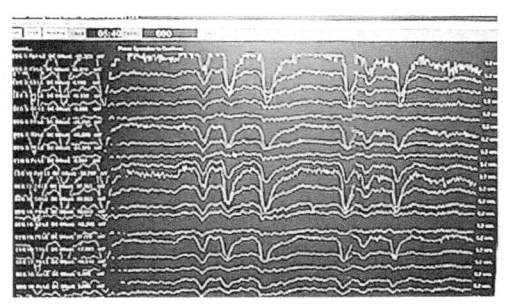

Brainwave measurement

results. Then the measurement session started. At first I was asked a few questions to check how my brain would react to them in terms of brainwave frequencies. Only later did I notice that these questions obviously served to put my mind into a very turbulent state in order to illustrate the difference between the state before and after measuring the institute's neurofeedback method. They asked me concrete questions like: "What was the worst moment or event in your life?" Immediately I thought about the moment when my father did not recognize me anymore due to Alzheimer's disease. He said to me, "Who are you? I don't know you." I also remembered other disturbing moments and, of course, I felt very sad and agitated after this question. That's when they immediately played some soothing music like a sonata of Mozart, which was sometimes intermediated by the sound of whales. The institute's specific neurofeedback method consisted of this specific combination of certain frequencies, which was supposed to put my brain in a balanced, coherent state. At this moment you may ask yourself: What exactly is a "coherent" brain state? You will find out soon, since we will discuss this in more detail in the following chapters of this book. For the time being, it is enough to mention that I indeed felt calmer and comfortable. Then, finally, I could chant for ten minutes in front of my compact mandala Gohonzon while my brain frequencies were measured.

An astonishing measurement result

I was waiting for the result. Were there some noticeable changes while I had been chanting? Could they detect any changes in my brain frequencies at all? When the responsible assistant of the institute showed me the results afterwards, I noticed that she seemed to have a deeply impressed and somehow shocked, astonished and almost bewildered expression on her face. Very soon I realized what made her so upset, when she presented to me the three different results of the measurements that had been taken.

The initial measurement that was taken while I was being asked certain disturbing questions showed continuously thick peaks, which indicated that my mind had been quite incoherent and agitated at that moment; the two halves of my brain were not working together in a harmonious way. The second measurement that was taken while I was listening to soothing music, and the measurements showed that the "jags" had been reduced by half. My mind had indeed become more balanced and coherent.

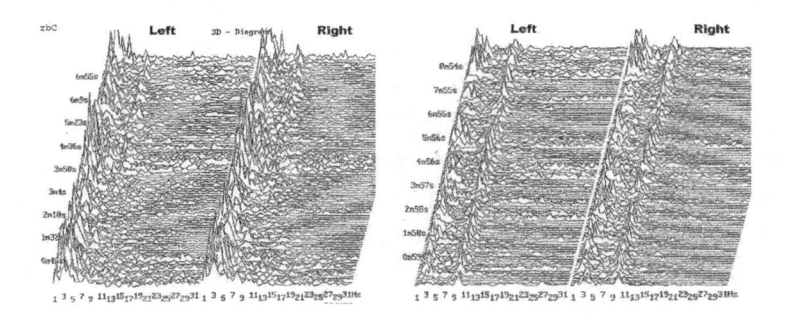

Brainwave measurement during questioning (left) and measurement during calming music (right)

But now I was in for a real surprise. The assistant showed me the result of the measurement that had been taken while I was chanting daimoku for ten minutes. It was amazing! The picture showed a perfectly balanced and even pattern; both the peaks and the zigzag shapes had completely disappeared. I was completely surprised and quickly realized that my short daimoku session had been proven to be effectively calming, even more so than the Institute's own neurofeedback method. My measurement showed the level of calm that the institute hoped to achieve, but its music-frequency method would require a few months of intensive training to achieve the result that I had showed after just ten minutes of daimoku!

The assistant immediately took the measurement result out of my hand. I asked her whether I could have it back and she told me that she could not give it to me. This had only been a test, and she couldn't release the results. If I wanted to undertake a more comprehensive measure in the future, then we could arrange that and I could take those results with me. I told her that the current test result was really fine for me and that I would pay her some extra money if necessary. I had just wanted to know whether any change in brainwaves during daimoku chanting could be measured, and whether there were certain significant changes or not.

But she vehemently refused to give me the test result. If those recordings were published, they would clearly show that ten minutes of daimoku were twice as effective than the institute's own method. The institute's method had been developed by the owner of the institute over many years and has been very successfully implemented in treating ADHD (Attention deficit hyperactivity disorder), learning disabilities, autism, Asperger syndrome (developmental disorder of social interaction), epilepsy, bipolar disorders (manic depression), excessive anxiety, sleep disorders and many more.

In the end, the institute's assistant offered to refund my whole payment, she was that determined to withhold the results. That's why we cannot show you the results here in this book. However, just imagine that there are no more thick peaks or zigzags on the picture of the previous measurements. Ten minutes of **daimoku** had produced very even lines that indicated that my brain had been in a coherent and harmonious state. From this moment on we definitely knew:

> **Daimoku** can put your brain into a harmonious state.

Does daimoku change your brainwaves?

You may have often experienced that chanting **daimoku** changes your emotional and physical state of life and expands the level of your consciousness. Whilst chanting you may perceive a strong energy rising from the bottom-up, an enormous clarity in your head while your restless thoughts have disappeared. That's when you feel full of energy, joy and optimism again. In this state I often see people smiling and their eyes sparkling.

By measuring our brainwaves when chanting **daimoku**, we wanted to get more information concerning this kind of transformation we experience every time that we chant. Is there any connection between a successful way of chanting **daimoku** and a specific pattern of your brainwaves? What kind of brain frequency should we achieve when we are chanting, in order to successfully change our reality? Is it possible to explain the implication of certain terms like "activating your Buddhahood" or of taking part in the "Ceremony in the Air" (as depicted in the Gohonzon) in neuroscientific terms?

We asked ourselves all these questions, constantly looked for an answer. That's why in September 2015 we visited another neuroscientific institute for further brainwave testing whilst chanting. We will discuss the results of this measurement in detail in the next chapter. Beforehand, however, we would like to give you some knowledge about brainwaves in general. At first there was the question: What kind of different brainwaves are there and what is their specific effect?

What are brainwaves?

In recent decades neuroscientists have discovered that our brain produces measurable brainwaves. All day long and even at night, the nerve cells in your brain communicate with each other and generate electrical impulses that fluctuate rhythmically in patterns called "brainwave patterns."

It is important to know that all humans display five different types of electrical patterns, or "brainwaves". The brainwaves can be measured and recorded with an EEG ("electroencephalograph"). Each brainwave has its own effect and contributes to optimal mental functioning.

The individual brainwave patterns are closely correlated with your thoughts and your emotions. They change depending on how alert or how tired you are, but also how calmly or emotionally you react to things and how much you can concentrate. Positive and negative feelings are also associated with certain brainwave patterns. This means that the rhythm of your brain is influenced by your feelings. Fear, worry, loving thoughts, hateful scenarios, stress – they all change your brain frequency and affect your body.

Each state of life, in the form of negative or positive thoughts and emotions, is associated with a certain brainwave pattern.

There are five major types of brainwave patterns. Our brain produces gamma, beta, alpha, theta and delta waves at the same time. However, depending on our prevailing emotions and thoughts, a certain state dominates. Your brain frequency also indicates how strongly you are connected to your subconscious mind.

Each of these brainwave patterns is associated with a particular state of consciousness.

Thus, our respective living conditions are accompanied by an interplay of certain brain frequencies. Let´s have a look at each of these brainwave patterns.

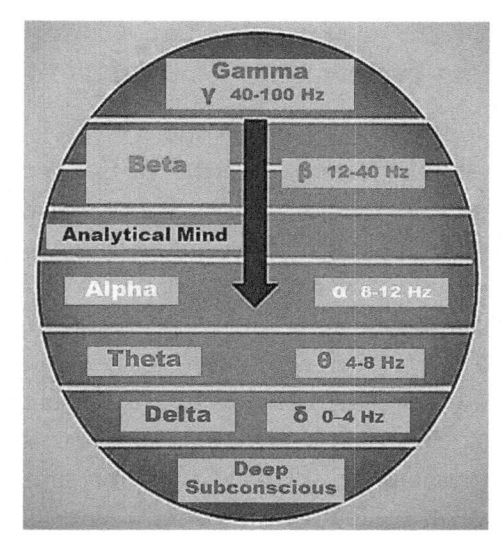

Different types of brainwaves

Gamma brainwaves: learning and storing new information

Gamma brainwaves are the fastest of brainwaves that oscillate between 40 to 100 times per second (a high frequency of 40-100Hz). They are considered essential for the simultaneous processing of information from all parts of the brain. They are present in sensory-binding, learning new information and storing memory. Gamma was dismissed as "spare brain noise" until researchers discovered it was highly active when you are in a state of universal love, altruism, and "higher virtue". It is speculated that gamma rhythms modulate perception and consciousness, and that a greater presence of gamma also relates to expanded consciousness and spiritual emergence. It has been found that individuals who are mentally challenged and have learning disabilities tend to have lower gamma activity than average.

Beta brainwaves: from focus to anxiety

The second most rapid pattern is called a beta brainwave pattern (13-30Hz). Beta waves are those that fluctuate between 12 and 30 times per second. This is the brainwave pattern of your normal, everyday consciousness. It is active when you are thinking logically and it tends to have a stimulating affect.

Having the right amount of beta waves allows you to focus and complete your work-based tasks easily. Having too much beta, however, may cause you to experience excessive stress and anxiety. The higher beta frequencies are associated with high levels of arousal. When you have a coffee or another stimulant, your beta activity will naturally increase. Think of beta waves as being very fast brainwaves that most people exhibit throughout the day in order to complete conscious tasks such as: analytical thinking, writing, reading, and socializing.

When you are predominantly in beta, your attention is directed outwards and identifies perfectly with the outside world. In this brainwave state, you have no access to your subconscious mind.

Highest levels of focus

Beta brainwaves increase your ability to focus and to get things done. People with a low level of beta often lack energy and have problems focusing on what they are doing. In a high beta state, you can easily generate positive thoughts and have less "mental fog".

To be effective in everyday consciousness

When you are in high beta brainwaves, you are able to think fast and generate new ideas quickly. Quick thinking definitely helps you in your job or when preparing for exams. Thus, beta brainwaves help you to increase your performance in everyday life.

Although there are many good things related to beta, problems can start when there is too much beta. If you increase beta when you already have a high level of it, you may quickly experience negative effects of too much beta activity.

High beta: stress and fear in everyday consciousness

At their highest, most rapid level (22-50Hz), beta waves are associated with anxiety, stress, disharmony, and disease.

Do you sleep badly? When you think of your boss, is your stomach contracting? Are you worried about the future? Is one of your colleagues stabbing you in the back to get your position? Are you worried about the economic or political situation in your country? Are you thinking how tomorrow you will have to endure a particular horrible colleague again who always puts himself in the center? Is your child ill and you don't know what the results of his medical examination will show? Do you still have to bring in more income for your firm this month, otherwise your job will be in danger? You are worried and anxious. Your brainwaves are in high beta!

People with excessively high beta brainwave activity are likely to suffer from anxiety, irritability, agitation, insomnia, bipolar tendencies, and substance abuse. This is one of the reasons why *slowing yourself down* from these faster beta waves can be very beneficial to you.

You are thinking too much

There are thousands of uncontrolled and constantly changing thoughts in your head. In such a situation it is difficult to concentrate on something for longer periods. Are you restless, can no longer think in a creative way and cannot find peace of mind? Are you addicted to the internet and find it difficult to sleep at night? That's when you are in high beta.

If you are too busy analyzing your situation, trying to find a solution, then your brainwaves are in high beta!

In the short term, such an over-focused attention span is useful because you can handle many things. This brainwave pattern, however, will cost you tremendous energy. When you have too much beta activity in your brain, your ability to solve problems shuts right down.

Your mind and your body are "upside down". You compete with others. You focus too much on something and it is very hard for you to stop it. As a result, you have sleeping problems, you are constantly tired, anxious or depressed. The solution is to find a way to slow down your brainwaves as soon as possible. This happens when you are able to enter the alpha state. Suddenly, all your stress and worry starts fading away.

Alpha-brainwaves: relaxation and clarity of mind

As long as you are at the level of your analytical mind, your brainwaves are in a state of high beta. It is only when you reach the alpha state that you start having access to your subconscious mind. This is why it is so important to get beyond your rational mind and to overcome the constant analyzing of your situation while you are chanting. This can happen as soon as your brainwaves slow down into the alpha brainwave pattern (8-12Hz).

Relax your body and clear your mind

In this condition you start relaxing and you are getting into a more uplifting mood. You are less preoccupied with all the external influences in your life. This means that you are no longer analyzing things and evaluating things too rationally any more. Tension and nervousness disappear as your brain's thought process is calmed down. Your mind becomes clearer.

When you are in the flow with daimoku

You're in a slightly meditative state. Deeply absorbed in what you are doing, like reading a good book or playing an instrument. You're so caught up in what you're doing that you've blocked out your awareness of what's going on around you. This happens when you are in alpha.

> In the alpha state, your inner world begins to become more real than your outer world.

Alpha brainwaves are also associated with joy, inner peace, and happiness. In alpha, you experience less stress and a greater sense of inner peace. Scientific research has shown that alpha is the primary brainwave pattern of meditation.

As you slow down your frequency, you start having access to your subconscious mind. But first of all, it is necessary to take your attention off the outside world. This happens when you are not thinking about your surroundings, your body or about time when you are chanting. You completely leave your old identity. This happens when you focus in a deep and concentrated way on the sign "myō", the third character from the top in the middle of the Gohonzon. As soon as your sensory impressions are significantly reduced, or whenever you just close your eyes once, your brainwave activity will automatically enter the slower alpha state.

Theta brainwaves: reprogram your subconscious

When your brainwaves slow down even further and you are deeply connected to your subconscious, you are in theta (4-8Hz). Theta waves fluctuate between 4 and 8 times per second. Theta brainwaves are slow and relaxing brainwaves. When you are dreaming at night, your brain is making much more theta waves than usual. When you are truly and deeply relaxed you are also in a state of increased theta brainwaves. In this state of consciousness, your perception is focused on your inner images.

Be more creative

Theta waves are associated with a state of additional, expanded awareness with which you have a broadened perspective on things. Suddenly you know the solution to a problem or see the whole picture of a situation. Researchers have also noted that the more theta waves you make, the more creative ideas you get to solve your problems. You see an option you did not see before.

In theta, you'll just see more than you see now. That's when you become more aware of your own patterns of thinking and feeling. Now you are able to act in a different way. The slower brainwave patterns are the brainwave patterns of increased awareness. When you have more awareness, you can stop responding automatically to people and situations around you. You see choices that you did not see in a more restricted state of awareness.

Reprogram your subconscious mind

In theta, you have deeper access to your subconscious and you are open to hypno-therapeutic programming because you are looking beyond the boundary between your awareness and your subconscious. However, it is seldom that adults predominantly experience theta brainwaves while they are awake. Children under the age of seven, however, experience this brainwave state on an ongoing basis. In theta, your brain is like a sponge. That's why children learn languages easily and soak in everything that you tell them without critical questioning. This is the way that children's brains are "programmed" and how their basic mindset and beliefs are set up. That's why it is so important to encourage children to develop a positive self-image like being confident and loveable.

> At this level, you have access to your subconscious.
> You can now start reprogramming.

Neutralize old traumatic experiences

The theta brainwave state is always associated with healing processes, because in this state you are connected to the power of your subconscious mind that is much greater than your everyday ego. The expanded state of awareness that you reach in theta provides relief from past emotional traumas. Researchers have found that people who remembered traumatic events while producing theta waves quite often experienced a resolution of the trauma. From then on, remembering the traumatic event no longer contained any emotional charge. It just appeared neutral, as if it had happened to someone else. It is as if you are just watching a TV drama with a certain inner distance. You might watch it, but you are not personally involved in it.

Delta brainwaves: healing and spiritual connection

When you go even deeper, you enter the delta state (0-4Hz). Delta waves are generally associated with dreamless sleep, which is the condition for deep healing processes and the strengthening of the immune system. It's possible, however, to remain alert in this state. That's when you are in a very deep, trance-like, non-physical state. Your conscious perception is restricted and a kind of "reset" takes place in your body. Your body starts regenerating. Most people aren't able to consciously experience the delta brainwave state. In deep meditation, however, this is possible.

Rejuvenate yourself

The delta brainwave pattern is associated with the deepest level of relaxation, causing your mind and body to restore after stress or after boosting your brain power. Thus, it is regarded to rejuvenate, replenish and heal your entire body and your brain.

Anti-aging effects

One of the associated benefits of increasing delta brainwaves is the release of anti-aging hormones. The delta brainwave pattern stimulates the release of beneficial substances like melatonin and DHEA, two powerful anti-aging hormones. This pattern also increases the release of human growth hormone. You make less human growth hormone as you get older, resulting in many aging symptoms like loss of stamina, and many diseases linked to aging. Spending time in delta quite possibly slows the aging process and keeps you young. If you remember, one of the meanings of "myō" is "to revive". To revive also means to heal in all aspects and levels of your life.

Is it possible to consciously experience delta brainwaves while chanting daimoku? Was this one of the reasons why we feel so relaxed, recovered and rejuvenated after chanting daimoku? We were wondering….

Increased compassion and intuition

Delta brainwaves can provide you with the ability to read other people's emotions and determine their feelings at an unconscious level. That's why increased delta brainwaves help you to have more compassion and understanding for other people. If you are very intuitive and always able to read other people's minds, you probably have more delta than the average person.

The deepest level of mind

Advanced meditation practices have associated the delta brainwave frequency with a feeling of all-encompassing bliss and with spiritual connection. This is the deepest level of mind. Someone called "a buddha" or "an enlightened person" may then be regarded as someone who has reached his or her deepest level of consciousness that corresponds to the delta brainwave state. In this state you are completely filled with unlimited compassion and wisdom.

Research in the field of meditation has shown that in this area you have access to the deepest level of your subconscious mind. According to Dr. Joe Dispenza, we are connected to the quantum field in this state. Therefore, at this level, information can also be transmitted over long distances between humans, because at this brainwave range you have access to the same field of information.

Meeting Dr. Joe Dispenza 2013 in the Netherlands

Connecting with universal life energy

Many meditation researchers also consider the delta brainwave pattern as a state in which you can connect your body and mind to universal life energy. Becoming consciously aware of experiencing the delta brainwave frequencies has been associated with the deepest sense of spirituality, the highest sense of internal awareness and feeling directly connected to a higher power.

The goal of advanced meditation

The goal of many meditation practices is therefore to increase the amount of slower brainwave patterns like alpha, theta or even delta brainwaves. After a lot of meditation practice, meditators are able to become consciously aware in the alpha and in the theta brainwave ranges. According to meditation researchers, it takes a lot of practice to cultivate awareness in the delta range. Experienced meditators, however, become more and more able to recognize and control their state of awareness and brainwave rhythms.

For us, the exciting question now was, in what way our brain frequencies would change while chanting **daimoku**? What exactly is the brain frequency at which transformation takes place? We wanted to find out and try this for ourselves. We had previously measured the energy of our bodies and the energy in the room that was produced by reciting ten minutes of **daimoku**. This time we just wanted to test the change of our brain frequencies that would occur during ten minutes of **daimoku**. In the long run, we want to carry out even more detailed investigations with many more people. For the time being, however, the question prevailed: What is the effect of ten minutes of intense **daimoku**? Was there any measurable change in our brain frequencies and therefore in our state of life?

Chapter 5

Shift your brainwave frequency with daimoku

> You have to be the change you want to see in the world.
> — Mahatma Gandhi

What changes occur during daimoku?

Sometime after our last experiment, we discovered that there was a neuroscience institute in the city where we lived. We went there to get some information. In order to find out what changes in our brainwaves occur when we chant daimoku, we decided to have various brain scans taken in real time while we were chanting. In addition, we wanted to have a brain scan taken *before* and *during* the daimoku mantra meditation with the help of an EEG. This way it was possible to measure how and if our brainwaves would change at all. This institute offered to measure and record our brainwaves with the help of two forms of EEG scan: a standard scan and a quantitative scan.

What is an QEEG?

An EEG (electroencephalogram) is a safe, non-invasive method to measure one's brainwaves using sensors fixed at up to 20 different points on one's head. Those kinds of brainwave measurements give you a lot of information about the current performance capacity of your brain. Physically the EEG sensors detect the minute electrical activity that is part of the normal functioning of one's brain

A measurement of brainwaves with a QEEG

A quantitative EEG, or QEEG (quantitative electroencephalogram) as it is called, is a specific form of analyzing an EEG measurement whereby the basic EEG activity is computerized into its individual frequencies and graphically represented. Measured EEG metrics such as frequency, amplitude and connectivity can thus be represented in the form of a so-called "brain map". This method is mainly used in the field of neuroscience, which examines neurofeedback, but can also be used in diagnosing and treating neurological or neuropsychiatric disorders.

What is brain mapping?

The institute we went to offered to take a QEEG measurement, which would measure 20 points of our heads and present the results in a brain map for us. The brain mapping translates the respective brainwaves into graphics that show color images that each correspond to a respective brain frequency. According to neuroscientists it is those frequency patterns that largely determine how we experience our reality.

The different color gradations presented in the brain map show how the brain activity recorded by the EEG corresponds to the average basic activity of the brain. A QEEG is a statistical measurement that shows whether a point is above or below average, and therefore how unusual the measurement is. It also provides information in relation to some demographics particular to the individual, like male or female and age, for instance.

The color red indicates when the brain activity is higher than normal, and the color blue indicates the areas where the brain activity is lower.

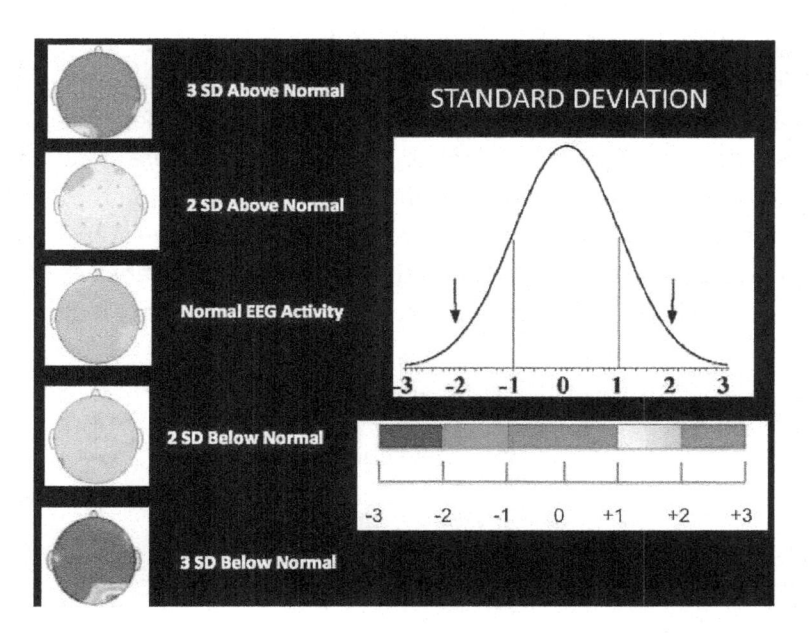

The various colors used in brain mapping

Measurement before chanting daimoku

At first, the neurofeedback expert took an initial measurement of my brain's usual frequency pattern. The result (see the Picture 1 on the next page) represents the state my brain was in when I had just sat down in the chair. Some thoughts went through my head, and I was a bit stressed out, because I had been stuck in a traffic jam for 20 minutes on my way, searched desperately for a parking space, and only just managed to get to the appointment on time.

While the neurofeedback expert was preparing the measurement, I wondered what would happen and whether it was possible to get some clear data. I thought having a brain scan on such a hectic morning would definitely show a very stressed image of my brain.

I was surprised when my results were evaluated: My brain scan showed an average and balanced brain, as one would expect before any mantra meditation. There were only a few small color gradations showing how strongly or how far my brain deviated from what is considered to be normal, balanced basic activity.

The few red lines in the brain scan indicate some minor communication above the normal range, which I was told were standard deviations. These were all the thoughts that were going through my head at that moment. The red lines in the beta range (12-15Hz) indicate some sensory-motor activities. That was not very surprising, for I had just looked at the compact Gohonzon that I had put up in front of me.

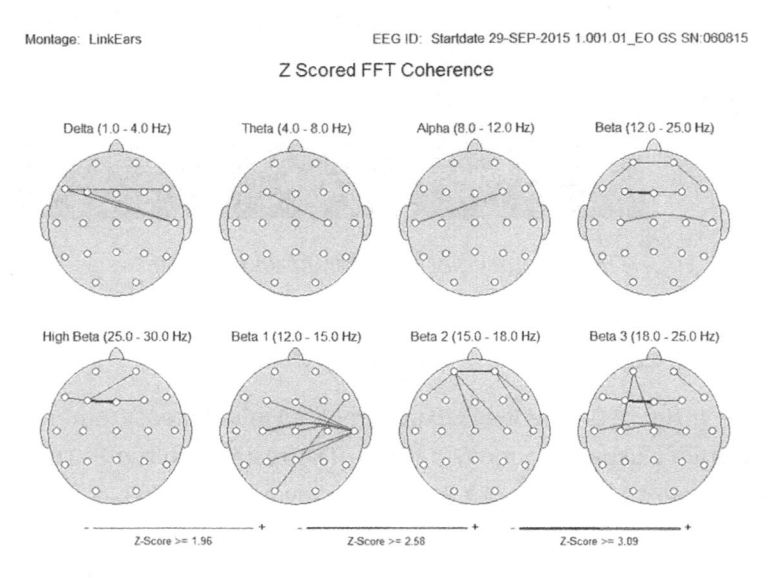

Picture 1: Brain mapping before daimoku chanting

The light blue lines in the high-beta range (25-30Hz) and the normal-beta range (12-25Hz) show that the high beta waves and the normal beta waves were slightly reduced, i.e. in this range my brain activity was lower than an average, basic state. This indicates that I had a tendency to be in a relaxed state. In its normal state, my brain was not as stressed out as I had expected it to be.

Train your brain fitness

The neurofeedback expert who took the measurement said that these results indicate that my brain had already been trained by some meditational practice for many years and that he thought that I was able to get my brain back into a relaxed state relatively quickly.

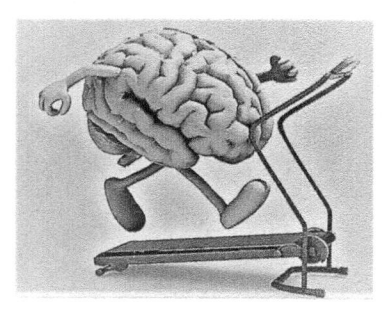

Train your brain fitness with daimoku

Until then, I hadn't really been aware that we could "train our brains", but that is exactly the case. Without knowing it, that's obviously what I had done with many years of daimoku practice. Unfortunately, only a few people are aware that our brains are changeable. We spend so much time and money on our physical fitness, but there is also the state of our brains, i.e. our "brain fitness" to take care of. As we shall see later, practicing daimoku is a very efficient way to do this.

Measuring brainwaves during daimoku meditation

I was really curious now. What changes would occur during the daimoku recitation to the Gohonzon? In which frequency range would my brainwaves be during the chanting? I had no idea. Then I chanted intensively just for ten minutes. The neuroscientist recorded the data of my brain activities while I was chanting and showed us the result later on. During the mantra meditation, considerable changes occurred in my brain. The results showed a strong increase in the slow brainwaves in the theta and delta range.

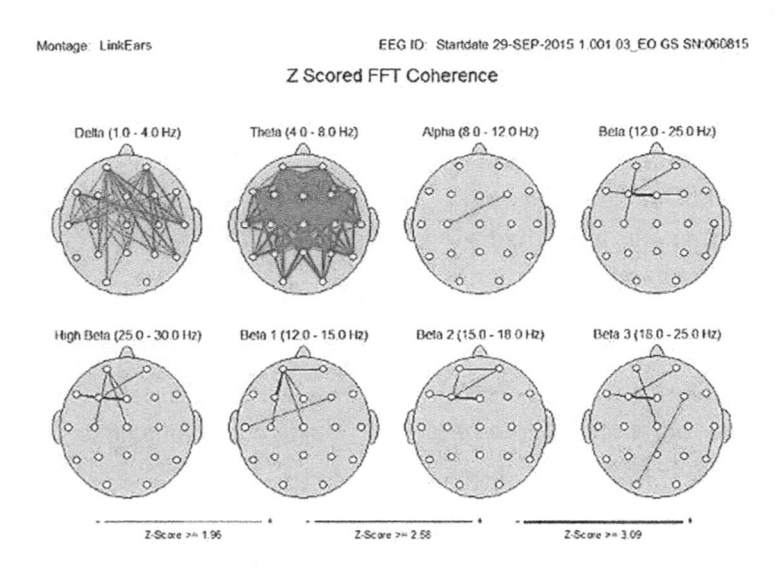

Picture 2: Brain mapping during daimoku chanting

Researcher and lecturer Joe Dispenza states that the higher and faster the brainwaves, the more we are in the conscious mind; the lower and slower the brainwaves, the deeper we are in the subconscious mind. Thus, I was in the deep layers of my subconscious mind during the ten minutes that I was chanting daimoku. It was very striking that during the daimoku meditation I was able to produce slower brainwaves in the theta and delta range, which according to meditation researchers indicate a state of deep relaxation and increased awareness. However, what did it really mean that there was such a strong increase in the coherence of the theta and delta brainwaves? What does coherence actually mean?

What is brain coherence?

When brainwaves slow down, something quite interesting happens in the brain: The two sides of the brain begin to communicate more with each other in a harmonious way. This is a result of a process called "brain synchronization", or brain coherence.

You might ask yourself: What exactly is brain synchronization? Well, first of all we have to recall that our brain has two halves, known as hemispheres. The amazing thing is that both halves of the brain often produce different brainwave patterns. This means that each hemisphere may have different type and level activity from the other at any given time. This is normal. If these brainwave patterns are too different, however, they are not in sync. They are incoherent. This is when your brain is in ego-mode and you don´t feel very harmonious.

Whenever we produce increasingly slow brainwaves, however, the brainwave patterns of the two cerebral hemispheres get more and more synchronized and oscillate at the same frequency. This is when they are working in unison, or in coherence; the more so, the more the different areas of your brain as a whole work together to form an integrative system. In principle, coherent brainwaves are a sign of a balanced brain, known as "whole brain synchronization".

In this state the two halves of your brain have coherent and symmetrical brainwave patterns. Our measurements have shown that this is exactly what happens when you chant **daimoku**. There was an increase of coherence, i.e. an increase of coherent brainwaves, in the theta and delta range.

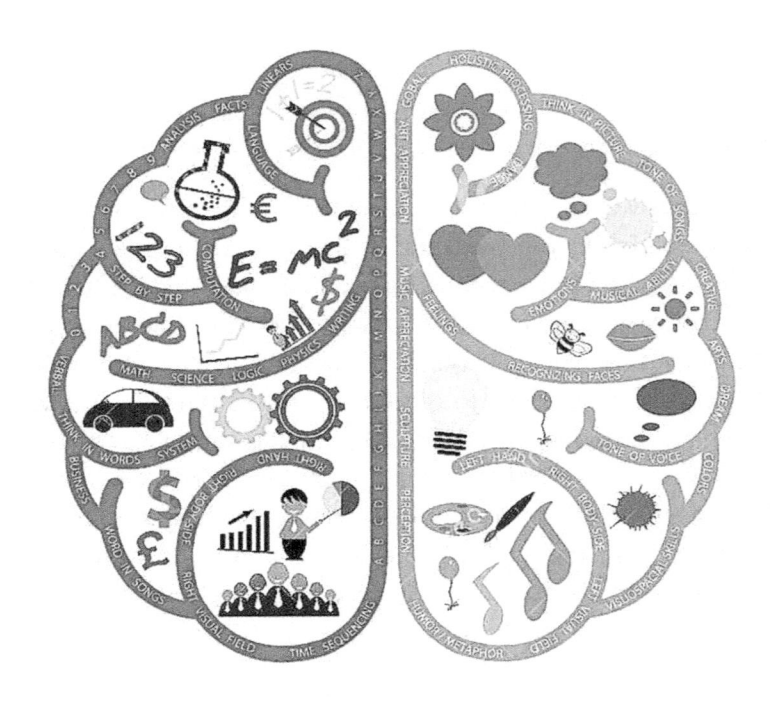

The left and the right halves (hemispheres) of your brain

A state of deep transformation

According to world-known meditation researcher Dr. Joe Dispenza, such an increased coherence in the theta range during meditation is an indication that a deep learning process, a personal healing process or some personal transformation is taking place.

Our neurofeedback expert himself was very surprised about the measurement results of our brainwaves while we were chanting daimoku. He said that the results showed the typical pattern of a "trance state". The surprising thing to him was that, quite on the contrary, I had actually been wide awake, in a highly focused and concentrated state. He had expected that the mantra meditation would increase coherence in the alpha range at most, since alpha is the state of relaxation when we pay less attention to the outside world and start to focus more intensely on our inner world. In the alpha state, we are in a state of imagination and daydreaming. That's when our inner world is more real than the outer world.

According to Dispenza, however, it is even more difficult to get down to the theta state during meditation. Theta is usually a kind of twilight state when we are half awake and half asleep. Dispenza considers theta to be the aim of meditation, for in this brainwave pattern we are deeply in our subconscious, because the analytical mind is not "in service".

> The theta state is also considered to be
> "the key to the kingdom of our subconscious mind".

Your brain is like a sponge

According to Dispenza, in the theta state the suggestibility of the brain is at its highest, in a form of hypnotic, receptive state. Every intention or image and vision generated in this state is directly imprinted onto the subconscious and stored there. Therefore, I was obviously deeply in a meditative state in the subconscious while I was clearly focusing on the Gohonzon and actively chanting. That seemed like a contradiction even to the neurofeedback expert who took the measurement, because he could not explain that the measurements clearly showed that technically I was in a state of trance, whereas I had my eyes open and was actually fully awake at the same time. It was something he had not come across beforehand. However, my brain was definitely in the state of theta.

As soon as the brain is predominantly in the state of theta, the hormone LTP is produced that enables heightened memory storage. Thus, what we learn in the state of theta remains in our memory and we can easily incorporate new visions and content into our consciousness, which then will remain there. Thus, the vision you have about your life when you are in the theta state while chanting, will remain in your memory, waiting to fulfill itself.

> In theta you become a sponge, easily soaking up information.

Your **daimoku** practice enables you to get into a coherent state of alpha or theta brainwaves. In those states, you will be far more susceptible to suggestion. Use this condition to focus on a specific goal.

> While chanting, you tap into the role of the creator of your life by going deep within and consciously choosing who you are, what you want to be and in which direction you are going.

Program your reality in theta

According to meditation researchers, it is possible for you to break out of the cycle of thoughts and feelings that constantly repeat your past when you are in a coherent theta state. In theta, you begin to notice a greater band of reality that you did not notice before. You suddenly realize options of which you were not aware before.

In this receptive state of theta, you can imprint your own personal goals directly onto your subconscious without your own intellect getting into the way. For in this state you have already left your everyday ego behind.

Thus, **daimoku** enables you to get into a coherent state of alpha and theta brainwaves. In order to achieve a certain goal, you can do your visualizations once you have reached a deep connection with the Gohonzon when you don´t think about who you are or what to cook for dinner tonight any more.

> There is one thing the subconscious mind cannot do:
> It cannot distinguish between what is real and what you are envisioning. Therefore, it tries to put into practice whatever you are holding in your subconscious mind.

Any positive imaging that you do in a state of theta while chanting will put your visualizations on "autopilot". For your brain, this will be a real experience.

Solve your problems in theta

You can also ask questions to tap into your intuition and solve problems, such as, "What do I have to do today to get that job?" In this state, you are also more receptive to clear intuitions by suddenly "knowing" what you need to do in order to achieve your goal. When you ask a question, or visualize a goal after reaching the theta state, do not be impatient. Intuitions may come within a few seconds or minutes, or they may come the next day. They will manifest more quickly the more you practice **daimoku**. The key is to let go and allow these things to come up.

Transform your emotions in theta

Research has shown that in the theta brainwave state positive emotional states are experienced even more intensively, and negative emotions are transformed into positive emotions. Many meditators also report that in this state they have very clear access to their real feelings and perceive themselves more authentically. That´s exactly what I experience every time that I chant intensively. Every time, I feel an incredibly clear and energizing feeling rising up from the bottom of my body.

Heal yourself in theta

Theta brainwaves also have a positive effect on your health – just as slow delta waves are associated with an improved immune function. Regular meditation in a theta state also leads to a reduction of stress-related symptoms, such as high blood pressure, headaches and susceptibility to infections. That´s because in this state the brain produces many endorphins that reduce any kind of stress reaction. At the same time, the amount of the stress hormone cortisol is also reduced.

All these fantastic reactions in your brain happen because theta strengthens the parasympathetic nervous system and thus soothes the sympathetic nervous system that is responsible for the "fight or flight reaction". In the theta state, there is a balance between these two opponents which gives us more physical energy and leads to better clarity.

Theta contributes to healing and health!

Our measurements have shown that the stressful condition of your brain caused by an incoherent brainwave pattern and which is often prevailing in everyday life can be dissolved by even a short daimoku meditation. According to latest research, stress is the biggest enemy to health. Cell researcher Dr. Bruce Lipton stated that stress is the cause of at least 95% of all disease. Therefore, it is very beneficial to be able to reduce your stress level with daimoku. But there is even more emotional relief awaiting us in this state.

Transform your blockages and beliefs

Recent meditation research reports that theta brainwaves enable you to recognize your own beliefs and blockages that hinder your personal development. Thus, they can be simultaneously transformed and deleted. Investigations have revealed that deep mental traumas are transformed by the state of theta in such a way that later on they might still be present as a memory, but they no longer provoke any emotional tension.

In the same way, the genetically inherited information of our ancestors is transformed and loses its burdening effect. When I read this, I suddenly realized why I could really change my karma when I chant daimoku. I also understood why I felt less stressed out by things, people or situations that used to do so.

> The measurements made it clear:
> By chanting daimoku, we can go beyond our thinking mind
> and relatively easily tap into the theta state
> where we can rewrite the programs in our subconscious.

Get access to unlimited pure consciousness

However, chanting daimoku takes you even deeper than theta and this is where you have access to the unlimited, enlightened pure consciousness. This is where real change and deep healing happens. This is like coming home to the natural state of your mind. At this level, you have access to all information ever stored and to unlimited life energy.

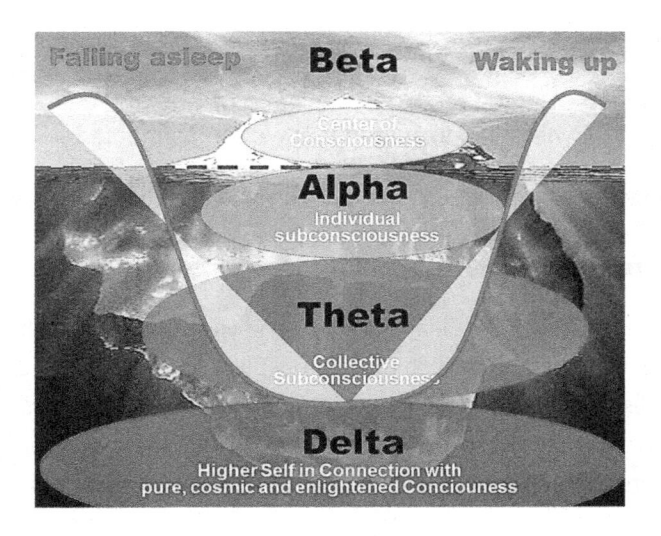

Illustration of brainwave levels

During the ten minute daimoku session we had measured increased coherence both in theta *and* in delta. According to Dispenza, increased coherence in the delta range is linked to the deepest level of consciousness at all: The quantum field, or the cosmic consciousness.

Coherence in delta is an indication that the focused daimoku meditation creates a connection to cosmic consciousness which, in Nichiren's metaphorical language, corresponds to participating in the Ceremony in the Air, as we discussed in our book *Transform Your Energy: Nichiren Buddhism 3.0*.

Following Dispenza´s statements, at that moment I was connected to a kind of "hyperspace", as it is called in quantum physics, consisting of pure consciousness. The connection to pure consciousness leads to a deep cleansing and transformation of our karmically-conditioned consciousness. This is the deepest level of transformation.

For Dispenza, this connection to the quantum field, as he calls it, is a very real connection. This happens when your brainwaves are very coherent in delta. That's when you're connected to your Higher Self. This is where true freedom starts.

> Chanting daimoku enables us even to tap into the delta state, where it is assumed that we are connected to cosmic consciousness.

Connect to the source of all being

Practicing daimoku is all about changing your own karma. In order to do so we need access to the deepest level of consciousness, our inner light, pure consciousness. This increase in awareness allows us to freely choose a new vision for our life. At the level of our restricted everyday consciousness we have no choice and we are subject to the law of karma. Here we may have the choice of choosing chocolate ice cream or vanilla ice cream as a dessert, as the well-known quantum physicist Amit Goswami put it. Otherwise, however, we find ourselves always exposed to our karmic patterns and experience similar situations again and again.

> You only really have two choices:
> You either connect to your spiritual side and re-create your life;
> or you are reactive and remain subject to old karmic patterns.

A prerequisite for the fulfillment of our desires is that we first reach the level of the expanded, enlightened consciousness, on which we are free from the karmic limitations of our lives. But how do we come to this level? Nichiren has shown us the way.

How do you know whether you are connected or not?

But how do we know that we are connected to cosmic consciousness? As soon as we completely "merge" with the Gohonzon, we no longer think about our environment, we no longer sense our body consciously in space. Once we are really deeply focused, we also forget time and later on we have no idea how long we have been in this trance-like state. That's when we are no-body, no-thing and no-time. That's when we are pure consciousness.

> We are absolutely present, we are in a state of coherence!

Chapter 6

Brain synchronization with daimoku

> Great universe has rhythm. Every rhythm of an individual life resonates with the rhythm of the universe. I think that "living" is "resonance" between the universe and our life, the microcosm. With the word "rhythm", the universe itself plays a rhythm. That's the "rhythm of mercy to make all living beings grow and improve." Or perhaps you should say "wavelength" of mercy. Life is a "receiver" that can catch this wavelength. Wherever you are, if you match the channel of the Buddha state, you will be filled with the melody of compassion for the growing of yourself and others. – Daisaku Ikeda
> on the "Emergence of the Treasure Tower" in:
> *The Wisdom of the Lotus Sutra (2000)*

Coherence is the magic word

Coherence is the key to having access to the *Ceremony in the Air*. In our book *Transform Your Energy – Change Your Life"* (NB 3.0) we described the Ceremony in the Air as a spiritual plane at the level of cosmic consciousness beyond time and space, where everything exists as a potential or as an energetic frequency pattern. This is the level where we have the choice to begin to re-create our lives. In order to get there, however, we first need the appropriate frequency. It's like a radio station: the frequency of this station is always there, but as long as you're not tuned in, you can't hear the music being played there.

> Creating coherence by synchronizing your brain with **daimoku** is the necessary condition for changing your karma, creating a better reality, health and success!

In the last chapter, we described in detail how we measured changes in the electrical activities of the brain during daimoku chanting. These electrical activities can be compared with a group of drummers. Let's not forget that there are two halves of the brain. If the frequencies of these two brain halves do not match harmoniously, then we are in a state of stress. When we are stressed, it is as if the drummers are playing out of sync with each other. That's incoherence. In this case, the brainwaves of our two cerebral hemispheres are very much in disorder and they are not coherent at all. We can imagine coherence as a rhythm or order and incoherence as a lack of rhythm, order, and synchronicity.

If, however, a few professional drummers are added to this group who are able to add a very orderly rhythm, as Joe Dispenza explains it, then the other drummers gradually come into a synchronous and orderly rhythm as well. Coherence therefore means consistent rhythm, or order, while incoherence is a lack of harmonious rhythm and order.

> Chanting daimoku is like an excellent drummer
> who gives the tempo and rhythm needed
> to get the brain's "orchestra" into harmony.

Balancing the left and right brain hemispheres

Thus, the principle of coherence applies to our brain. Usually we think of our brain as a united whole. We forget that we have two different brain hemispheres, each of which can have a completely different orientation to the other.

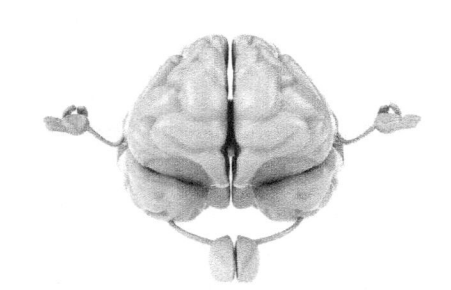

The right side of the brain is responsible for emotional, intuitive and creative processes, while the left side "thinks" rather logically, rationally, and analytically.

In the middle, below the two brain hemispheres, is an essential point that combines the two: the corpus callosum. This is the thin white strip that connects the left and the right hemisphere of your brain.

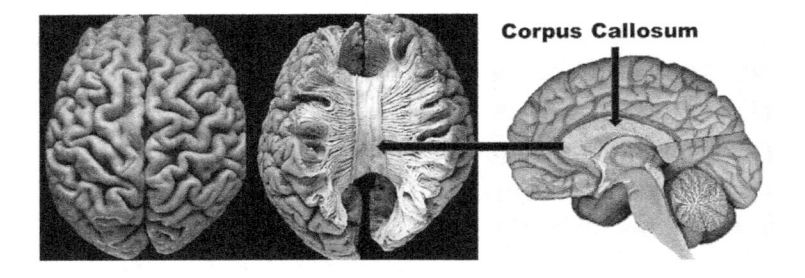

Corpus Callosum

Thus, the two brain hemispheres are linked by the corpus callosum through which they communicate and coordinate actions and decisions. It was discovered by Roger Sperry, who was awarded the Nobel Prize in Physiology and Medicine in 1981, that each hemisphere of the brain has its own separate and specific function. Thus, coordination and communication between the two hemispheres is absolutely essential. It turns out that the corpus callosum is literally the bridge between your critical mind and your creative mind. It is the connection between that part of you that likes to think about the past and worry about the future and the other part of you that is present right here, right now. It has been known for a long time that meditators have thicker corpus callosums than non-meditators. Now research knows that the longer you are able to reach a whole brain state as was shown in our measurements while we were chanting daimoku, the thicker this corpus callosum becomes. This means the next time you are in a stressful high demand situation you will have better access to the creative problem-solving part of you, that present moment awareness. Therefore, chanting daimoku prepares you for finding a solution to your everyday problems. For having this connection between your creative and your critical mind allows you to come up with a solution when, for instance, you are facing a stressful situation at work. Since you are accessing more areas of your brain, it is easier for you to meet this demand.

Chanting daimoku creates a bridge
between your critical mind and your creative mind

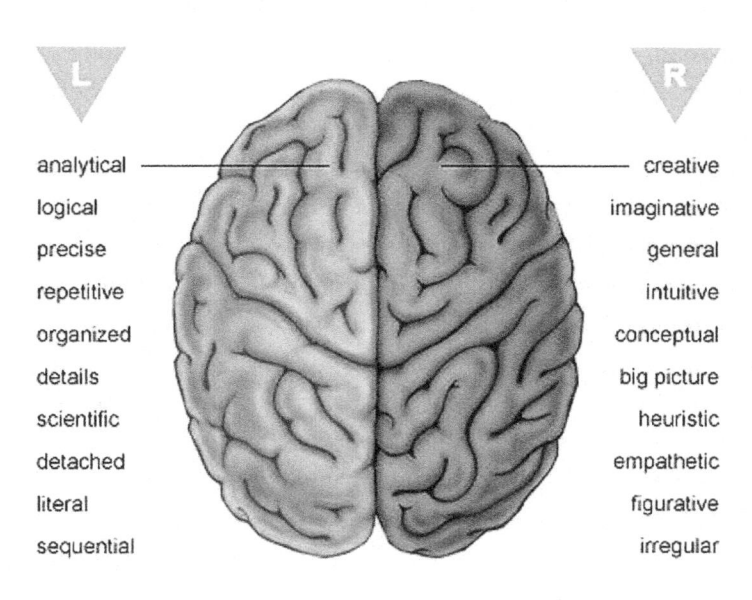

L		R
analytical		creative
logical		imaginative
precise		general
repetitive		intuitive
organized		conceptual
details		big picture
scientific		heuristic
detached		empathetic
literal		figurative
sequential		irregular

The left and right halves of the brain

Your critical mind and your creative mind

Logically-minded people who predominantly use the left hemisphere are generally more practically-oriented or good at math's and natural sciences. Creative people, on the other hand, who mainly use the right hemisphere, often tend to act more intuitively. Often among them are successful artists.

However, I was not really aware of how strongly these two completely different aspects of our two brain halves influence our perception until I happened to read the story of a renowned neuroscientist.

Dr. Jill Bolte Taylor is a Harvard-trained neuroscientist who suffered a massive stroke in the left hemisphere of her brain. In her book *My Stroke of Insight: A Brain Scientist's Personal Journey* she describes her unusual experience. When she had the stroke, she suddenly noticed that within four hours she could not sit still, walk, talk, read, write, or remember anything from her life. Bolte Taylor alternated between the euphoria of the intuitive and kinesthetic right brain, in which she felt a sense of complete wellbeing and peace, and the logical, sequential left brain, which recognized that she was having a stroke and enabled her to seek help before she was completely lost. It would take her eight years to fully recover.

Assigning the left hemisphere of her brain to the analytical ego and the right hemisphere to the holistic self, it was obvious that Bolte Taylor was more experiencing her holistic self, having full access to the right hemisphere of her brain as well. She seemed to be connected with the whole universe. After her stroke, time and space did not exist. She just saw magnificent, powerful energy. At the same time, she knew exactly what she was doing. Later Bolte Taylor completely recovered from her stroke and regained her usual sense of "self". Her experience, however, suggests that the state she experienced is in any one of our brains. It's a state of coherence that we can "tune into", when we are "at one" with everything and therefore can manifest wonderful things into our lives. It's that feeling of connection with all living things. When you are in such a coherent state you feel wonderful and at peace. Your interactions with your environment come from a place of power and trust.

Luckily you do not have to go through the trauma of a stroke in order to experience a state of coherence. But most important is that this state of coherence is the state in which we can bring the things we desire to ourselves.

> The good news is that you can always switch your frequency and connect to universal consciousness by chanting **daimoku** to the Gohonzon.

This is what our measurements have clearly shown. Maybe you have to switch your frequency constantly throughout the day, because you keep slipping back into the negative feelings and moods of a lower life state. That's normal. It is just like tuning into a different frequency. You have a tendency to fall back to your old frequency until the new frequency becomes stronger and has consolidated itself. One reason for this is that the two halves of your brain have probably been out of sync for too long.

When you are out of sync

Up to now, have you really been aware about the fact that you don't just have one brain, but two brain hemispheres? Both brain halves produce different brainwave patterns. That's normal. However, if these brainwave patterns are too different, they are not coordinated and in a state of incoherence.

The brainwaves of the two halves of the brain can be totally out of sync. That's when you are in ego-frequency, your brainwaves are in high beta and you feel disharmonious. Do you remember? High beta has shown to be prevalent when we are stressed, anxious, depressed and unwell.

Furthermore, we all know that people are either "left-brained" or "right-brained", i.e. that one side of the brain is more dominant than the other. This explains why some people tend to think more logically and others are more intuitive.

However, this is only the case in "everyday consciousness", when your brainwave patterns are predominantly in beta. In a beta brainwave pattern people are either very right brain dominant or left brain dominant. There is not much harmony between the two hemispheres of the brain and you have the tendency to feel stressed out.

When your brainwaves are out of sync

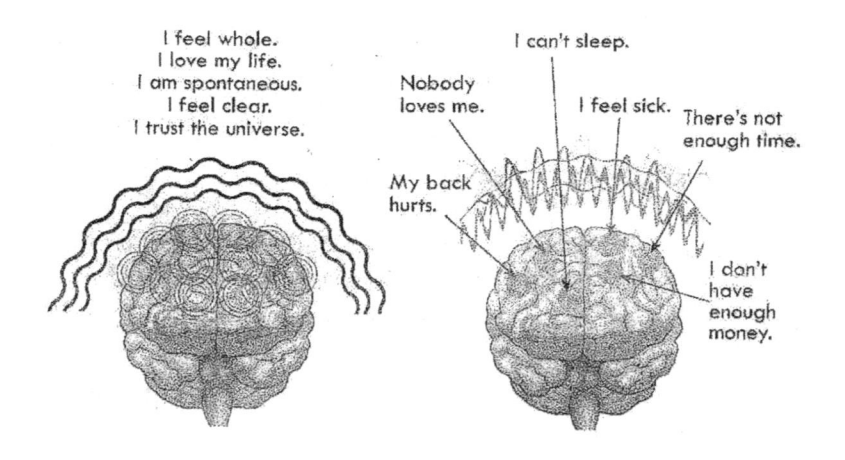

Source: Joe Dispenza 2012, p.209

The right-hand picture shows a brainwave state where there is no synchronicity between the two halves of a brain. When the two sides of the brain are engaged in different types of activity, then the signals measured from the two sides are dissimilar and out of phase. In this case there is little coherence between the two sides of the brain and there is little communication taking place between them. As mentioned before, that's when you feel depressed, anxious and chronically frustrated.

An incoherent brain makes you ill

The brain functions as part of the central nervous system that controls and coordinates all other physical systems in the body. Once the brain is in a state of incoherence, it also sends incoherent signals along the spinal cord into all other physiological systems of the body. Then the whole body gets out of balance and the result is diseases of all kinds.

If this happens continuously, stress with incoherent brain signals leads to depression, sleep disorders, heart rhythm disorders or hypertension, and the immune system is strongly weakened. A weakened immune system, in turn, leads to frequent and long-lasting colds, allergies, cancer, rheumatism and many other diseases.

The cause is an unbalanced nervous system, because the brain is too often in the high-frequency beta state that makes you focus too much on the 0.000001% reality of your outer world. Then you believe that this is the only possible reality, and that what your senses can detect is the only level of reality where you can change things. Your incoherent brain state, however, will be reflected in your outer life. You first have to change your brain frequency in order to change your outer situation. You need to change from the inside out.

> If your brain is working properly, then you are working properly.
> If your brain has more coherence, then you are more coherent.
> If your brain is more holistic and balanced, you are more holistic and balanced.   – Joe Dispenza

An incoherent brain causes stress and depression

Different streams of consciousness are constantly being processed in your brain. As we already described above, the electrical activities of a brain in a state of stress can be compared with an orchestra whose instruments are not matched to each other. But when is this actually the case? When is your brain in such an incoherent state?

According to German neuroscientist Gerald Hüther, your brain reacts with such an incoherent state when you experience the unpleasant feeling of being marginalized, bullied or punished by others. Then your brain gets out of balance.

To be excluded by others, for example, stimulates the same region in your brain that is activated when a person feels physical pain. In such a moment, the brain gets into an incoherent state, i.e., the brainwaves are not synchronized. No one can endure physical pain for a long time. Such a condition consumes too much energy. However, the pain of such unpleasant interpersonal experiences can only be alleviated if we are able to return to a coherent state in order to find some inner peace and calm. Here again, the power of **daimoku** is a great help.

When you are constantly worried or depressed, when your boss or partner annoys you, your brain also gets increasingly incoherent, which in turn causes even more depression and anxiety. If the two halves of your brain no longer work together harmoniously, then all other systems in your body won't work together either. That's when you are in the best condition for getting ill.

A coherent brain – the necessary condition for healing

Hüther argues that the brain always tries to establish a balanced state of coherence or synchronization because it consumes very little energy in this state. When the brain is in a coherent state, it sends decent, synchronized signals to the body and these signals bring all your body systems back into coherence, that is, into harmony.

This in turn affects the cardiovascular system, the digestive system, the immune system and all other systems. The nervous system is realigned and thus the vast amount of energy that until then has been simply put into survival and the processing of negative emotions is now available for creating something new. The body begins to heal. Now we have the energy to develop a new vision for our future. But how do we get into such a balanced, coherent state?

Do you feel overwhelmed?

Chanting is definitely aimed at improving your life. This includes your ability to handle the various stress factors in your life. There are certain ways to actually tell whether you are getting better at handling stressful situations in your life.

This basically means that when the two hemispheres of your brain are synchronized you are able to simultaneously hold many things in your awareness. This is valuable no matter what your job is. Whether you are running your own company or whether you are a stay-at-home mum, you have to be able to actually hold many things in your awareness at the same time. That is only possible when you are able to get rid of the stress in your body which has the effect of pulling the lens of your awareness aback so you create space in order to hold many things in your awareness at the same time. If you can't do this, you may easily feel overwhelmed just by having to solve one of the problems you are currently facing in life.

You are getting a wider perspective on things

Using chanting to synchronize your two brain hemispheres enables you to deexcite your nervous system. Thus, you are creating order in your body. When you create order in your body, the accumulated stress you have in your body cells can start to leave the body. The less stress you have in your body, the more conscious power you have for the task at hand for the right now.

As your brain synchronizes, there is more communication between the two hemispheres of your brain. As this happens, your awareness increases and you begin to develop a kind of extended awareness. This helps you to get a new perspective on things. It's as if you're looking at things from a bird's view. All of a sudden you look at things from a higher spot on the mountain, so to speak. You have a view of things you did not have before. Now you can see the whole picture of your situation.

You are able to detect patterns

In this state of extended awareness, when your brain is synchronized, you suddenly see the solution to a problem or see that you behave in a certain pattern that does not serve you.

Your awareness shifts from a narrow-minded, over-focused, obsessive survival mode into a more open, relaxed, holistic, present, orderly and creative way of thinking. This is actually our natural state of being.

In this state you have access to your subconscious mind. Your feelings are transcended and you forget your old ego identity. The deeper you merge with the Gohonzon, the more your attention shifts away from your environment, your body, and from time. Many impressions from outside no longer reach you inside. The electrical activity in your neocortex is reduced. The neocortex is that part of the cerebral cortex that is involved in sensory perception, conscious thought and language.

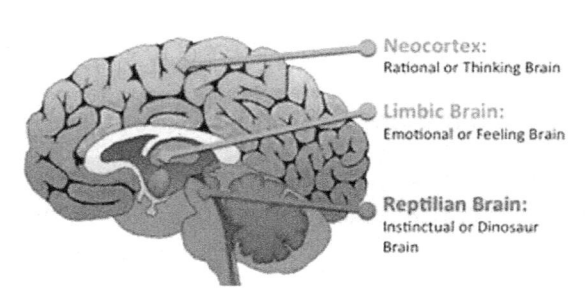

Neocortex:
Rational or Thinking Brain

Limbic Brain:
Emotional or Feeling Brain

Reptilian Brain:
Instinctual or Dinosaur Brain

This process calms down your analytical mind and your brain adjusts itself to a more ordered, coherent brainwave pattern.

Then you will feel connected, perfectly balanced and you experience healthier emotions of a higher frequency such as trust, joy and inspiration.

The longer I chanted, the more sensitive I became to the inner conditions of other people. I started to notice very quickly when their mind was restless and their two brain halves were not harmoniously connected.

Brainwave synchronization with daimoku

Only when we are able to synchronize our brain are new neural connections developed between the two brain hemispheres. This means that the more I chant, the more I strengthen the connection between the two brain hemispheres. Now I understood what the neurofeedback expert had meant when he said that he could see right away that my husband and I had been meditating for a long time because our brains were "balanced". I remember thinking that this was funny, because I wondered how he could actually tell whether my brain was "stressed" or "balanced".

What he meant was that even in a state of rest my two brain hemispheres already worked together harmoniously as a result of my chanting **daimoku** throughout the years, producing many new connections and unifying the analytical and creative sides of the brain.

I quite vividly remember that this is exactly what happened when I was writing my PhD thesis. Whenever I was chanting **daimoku**, I suddenly had ideas about how to structure the text I was writing or whom I should ask for advice. Every time that I felt stuck, I chanted intensively and that´s when the solutions came to me.

Improve your emotional stability

Our measurements indicate that you can enter a synchronized, balanced brain state while chanting daimoku. One of the signs that this is happening is an increase in your emotional stability. Every person has a certain emotional limit of what he or she can handle. If the events in your life push you over that limit, i.e. if emotionally you are trying to deal with something that is beyond your capacity, you begin to feel overwhelmed.

Once you are over your threshold, your negative emotions come up and you start to feel anger, confusion, fear, anxiety or depression. You might find yourself having a cigarette or a glass of alcohol, in order to slow down your brainwaves and to get into a more relaxed, balanced brain state.

When I started chanting, I realized that the threshold of what I can handle was very low. This was one of the reasons why sometimes I tended to be either angry, depressed, or anxious that something bad could happen.

My parents´ illnesses and the emotional stress I felt at not having a secure home to go to any more and for having a brother constantly trying to harm me were more than I could emotionally handle at the time. This insecurity and the feeling that I constantly had to fight for things triggered a lot of anger in me. Often people could trigger my anger button very easily. That´s because at the time I thought other people or my bad luck were responsible for my own feelings. The more I chanted daimoku, however, the more I became aware that this anger was *stored inside* me.

I chose to take responsibility for my life. I realized that it was something about me that I needed to change, because I wasn´t getting the results I wanted.

You get attracted to different situations

As soon as I started chanting, I was suddenly attracted to different situations and to people who had a more positive effect on my life.

I became more sensitive to situations and couldn't tolerate people that weren't serving me. I was more aware of my decisions. After a while I felt that I had more choice.

I felt a big change after I had been chanting for a while. My emotional stability had increased. The things that triggered me previously did not bother me that much anymore. It took a stronger trigger or it took much longer to get me into a state of anger, fear or depression. And once I got into those states, it did not take me as long to get out of them as it used to.

Be more relaxed about things

Chanting daimoku on a regular basis, you become more relaxed because you're less emotionally reactive. This was also one of the biggest changes that one of our participants noticed about herself since she started chanting. She told me that she and her whole family had noticed that the abusive behavior of her father-in-law didn't make her react with anger and the feeling of powerlessness to the extent that she used to. She handled the situation in a calm way and started to positively influence her family in this matter. She told me very often that without daimoku the whole situation would really get her down. Even her friends had noticed that she had become quite relaxed on certain matters recently. She realized that her reactions had become more "neutral" than before, as she put it. The anger had somehow melted away.

The driver in front of you, you partner, your neighbor, your boss, your colleague, your mother-in-law – whoever used to just drive you up the wall cannot get to you that easily any more, the more that you synchronize your brain with daimoku. As the above-mentioned practitioner put it: You realize that you make much better decisions and that, finally, you are happier.

The anti-aging effects of daimoku

In brain research, a coherent brain state is associated with reversing your own age process. In Japan I often saw people who had been chanting for many years, sometimes decades, and who seemed to be much younger than they actually were. There is even a Japanese term for this: they are said to have "hokke beauty".

The term "hokke" comes from the word "hokekyō", which literally means "lotus sutra" or "dharma flower". When people use this term, they want to say that someone who believes in the Lotus Sutra and practices it will increasingly radiate beauty and dignity. A coherent brain state might be one of the factors to explain the phenomenon of "hokke beauty".

Nichiren mentioned "prolonging one's life span" with daimoku. He managed to even prolong his mother's life by four years by chanting daimoku, as he explained in his own words in his gosho:

> When I prayed for my mother, not only was her illness cured, but her life was prolonged by four years.
> *On Prolonging One's Life Span (1279)*

In this gosho, he explains that one's life span is normally considered to be fixed karma, i.e. karma that cannot be changed. He indicates, however, that with the help of daimoku even fixed karma can be changed and your own life span can be prolonged.

Our measurement showed that chanting daimoku harmonizes the hemispheres of the brain, making communication of thoughts, information and responses more effortless and coherent. Since a more integrated system produces better mental and emotional health, it doesn't come as a surprise that the latest results in brain research regard such a brain state to be one of the most powerful "anti-aging" methods.

The secret to being successful

Most people unconsciously favor one side of the brain over the other, thus creating an imbalance. We can observe this: you soon have an idea whether the person you are dealing with responds to their environment in either more of a logical or an emotional way. There are, however, people who use both halves of their brain in the same way, and those people really differ from most other people.

> Studies on brain scans have shown that in the case of highly successful people, both brain halves work in unison.

If both halves of your brain can be synchronized, not only can the above-described disorders such as depression or deep-seated frustration and pain be reduced, but the thinking processes of the two brain halves can also become better coordinated with each other. This means that you think more holistically and you combine intuitive and logical elements, thus reaching a more comprehensive and effective way of thinking and acting.

A high level of coherence indicates that the two sides of the brain are networked, with a high level of inter-communication. A high level of brain coherence, as we measured it when chanting daimoku, has been correlated to a wide range of improved mental performance leading to more success.

A synchronized brain makes you a good leader

The neuroscientists Dr. Jeffrey Fannin and Dr. Robert Williams call a coherent state of the brain, where the two parts of your brain show symmetrical coherent brainwave patterns, a "whole-brain state", i.e. a bi-lateral, symmetrical brainwave pattern. The two scientists claim that a whole-brain state is fundamental to achieving sustainable success in one's life. Research indicates that successful leaders in private or in business use their brains differently than less-effective leaders. At this point you might ask yourself: In what way is the success I have in life related to my brainwave state?

Well, first of all the researchers regard this type of brain state as a required condition for making adequate decisions and to be a successful leader. How come? They say that you can only do this when you are not in a state of fear, worry or anxiety yourself. Various research results indicate that you can only successfully lead people, if you can arouse positive emotions within yourself that influence the group that you are trying to lead.

Fannin and Williams' research showed that both things can be achieved by entering into a whole-brain state. A more coherent brain is more creative, more intelligent and makes better decisions. A more coherent brain also helps you to handle change and uncertainty in an ever more demanding business world, thus allowing you to be more flexible. All these factors help you to improve your personal development for greater success.

Upon reading this I became deeply aware in the way that being successful was directly linked to my **daimoku** practice. A coherent brain state lets you react in a calm way, and makes you more flexible and positive.

Our measurements had clearly shown that I was able to enter a whole-brain state while chanting **daimoku**. I felt very positive afterwards. And you need to be positive in order to be successful. It is difficult to be focused and to motivate other people when you are depressed. Once again I started to deeply appreciate being able to chant **daimoku**.

I feel this effect every time I go to my company seminars on intercultural competence in international business. Before leaving the house before I give such seminars I always chant a lot of **daimoku**, because I am quite aware that the participants of my seminars reflect my own inner life state. I chant to be able to reach their hearts and to really give them something valuable for their lives when taking part in my seminar.

I have often experienced it myself that you have to be able to arouse positive emotions in a seminar and stay positive yourself in order to counteract the negative life state or emotions of some people.

There is a lot of research indicating that a coherent brain is the prerequisite for success and even provides the "ultimate competitive edge" in business, because leadership demands coherence. This is because a coherent brain makes the body healthier, more energetic and more resistant to stress which is one of the characteristics of a successful leader in business.

Leadership demands coherence

Research indicates that anybody who is trying to lead people must be able to counterbalance negative emotions and arouse a positive atmosphere. Brain coherence and integration, therefore, seem to determine the levels of transformational growth and leadership performance in a person.

This powerful influence of brain synchronization was revealed in 1988 in a study reported by researchers of the Universidad Nacional Autónoma de Mexico.

The report revealed that synchronized brain states significantly influence nonverbal communication with the people in your environment. The study was done with thirteen paired subjects. The subjects were tested in a darkened and soundproof Faraday cage that filtered out all outside electromagnetic activity. Each of the thirteen pairs was instructed to close their eyes and try to 'communicate' by becoming aware of the other's presence. Whenever one of them felt the other's presence they were supposed to signal the experimenter when they felt they did so.

At the same time, the brainwave states of all participants were monitored during this process. Experimenters reported that during the sessions, an increase in similarity of EEG (electroencephalographic) patterns between the pairs developed. Furthermore, the experimenters noticed that the person with the highest degree of brainwave synchronization was the one who most influenced the session.

This means that when your brain hemispheres are in a synchronized state, your brainwave pattern can automatically affect the people around you in a very positive way, even before you communicate verbally. This applies to your client, your partner, your child, your boss or your colleague. Thus, practicing daimoku improves your communication with other people before you even say a word.

Transform fear and worry

My daimoku practice made me more aware of when my brain was in an incoherent state, because practicing daimoku allowed me to experience a coherent brainwave state more often and feel the difference between the two states more clearly. After a while I began to understand why my feelings of fear were always transformed and removed when I was chanting daimoku. It has to do with the one part of your brain that is responsible for strong emotional responses: your amygdala. The amygdala is the integrative center for emotions, emotional behavior and motivation.

When does your amygdala get activated?

The body's alarm circuit for fear lies in an almond-shaped mass of nuclei deep in the brain's temporal lobe. The amygdala, from the Greek word for almond, controls autonomic responses associated with fear, arousal, and emotional stimulation and has been linked to neuropsychiatric disorders, such as anxiety and social phobias. There are normally two amygdalae per person, with one amygdala on each side of the brain. They constitute a part of the limbic system within the brain, which is responsible for emotions, survival instincts and memory.

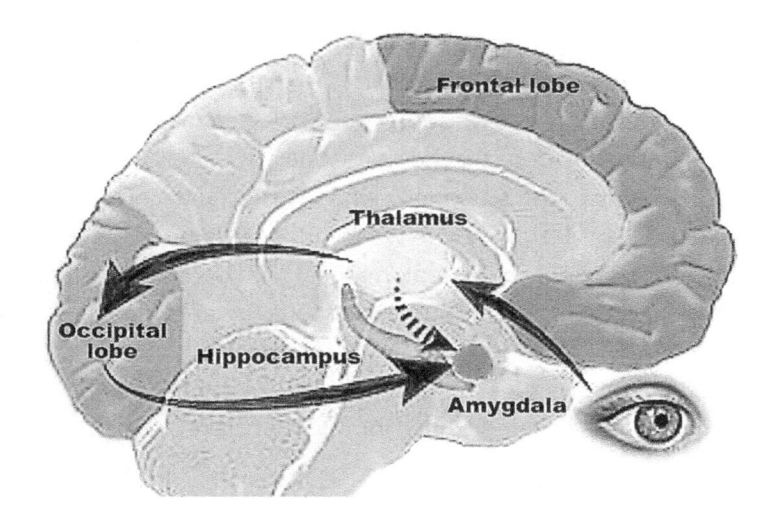

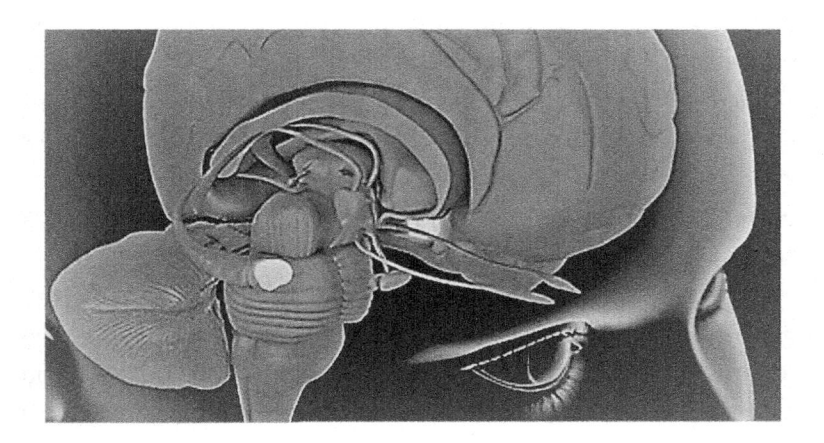

The amygdala is also responsible for the perception of emotions in other people, such as their expressions of anger, fear and sadness, as well as the controlling of aggression in the individual. It helps to store old memories of events and emotions so that a person is able to recognize similar events in the future. If, for instance, you were once let down by a good friend, your amygdala may be 'activated' and then make you anxious whenever somebody else's behavior reminds you of this event. If you were bitten by a dog when you were a child, your amygdala may still increase your fear and alertness around dogs today.

This happens to me personally whenever I see a German shepherd. Once I was bitten by one when I was 10 years old. Although I really do love dogs in general, my heart always starts pounding whenever I see a German shepherd coming towards me that is not on a leash.

Have you ever had fearful thoughts like "What if I get laid off"? or "My business is going to fail" or "I won't have enough money when I am old"?

These kind of self-defeating thought patterns will eventually over activate your amygdala and trigger a 'fight or flight' response, creating high levels of anxiety and fear at a subconscious level that negatively impact your behavior and your productivity. This in turn affects other brain regions as well.

One of those regions is the frontal lobe, where many important decisions are processed. That's why it is essential to be able to interrupt such fearful emotions when you have to make important business decisions and when you are trying to lead a group of people, for instance.

Whenever you feel insecure or threatened by any perceived danger, your amygdala is activated. If you leave your secure job to start your own business and you become anxious that you might fail, your amygdala gets activated immediately, making you even more anxious. Whenever you ask yourself whether you are able to sell enough products in order to keep your job, your amygdala starts reacting. Whenever you listen to the media predict some new financial and economic crisis, your amygdala gets activated, if you are scared by such news. Now your subconscious fears are spinning even when you are thinking about other things. It is a vicious circle you can hardly stop.

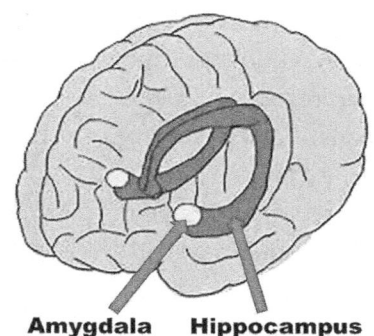

Amygdala   Hippocampus

Fear stops your motivation

The latest research in neuroscience reveals that you can condition your brain, through chronic worry or fear, to believe that the world is unsafe. When this happens, your motivation completely shuts down, and neurons throughout your brain begin to disconnect from each other. Your mental clarity and problem-solving skills are reduced, your confidence drops, and you find it difficult to act properly in any social situation.

Avoid amygdala attacks

In the long run, the subconscious patterning of your fearful thoughts will make you focus on looking out for even more danger. Scientific experiments found that when fearful facial expressions were shown in a way that people did not consciously know they had seen them, the amygdala was still activated. This means that subconsciously you detect the fearful emotions of other people, which will also activate your amygdala and make you anxious as well.

Several studies have shown that the amygdala modulates the fear response in humans. Fearful stimuli including fearful faces, fear-inducing images, and fear-conditioned cues, have been found to activate the amygdala in several brain imaging studies using positron emission tomography (PET).

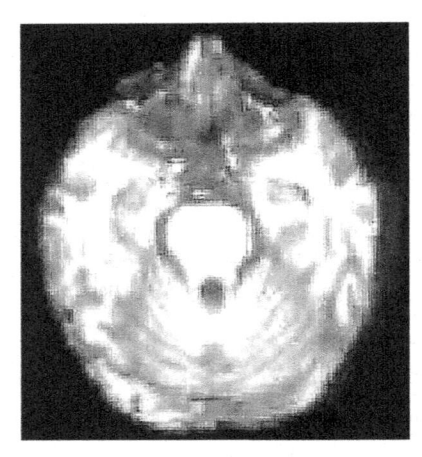

The amygdala responds to fear by lighting up in this positron emission tomography brain scan. Wellcome Dept. of Cognitive Neurology / Science photo library

However, there is a solution. Researchers demonstrated that entering into a whole-brain state will move your brain out of this negative default mode and calm down your amygdala. Now you have access to more resourceful thinking processes. This is precisely what happens when you chant daimoku. As our measurements have shown, you can enter into a whole-brain state while chanting. I had learned why my anxious thoughts and my fearful scenarios stopped whenever I chanted daimoku. Not only did they stop but they gave way to a soothing, positive and energetic feeling of optimism and motivation.

Calm your fear center

Known as the anxiety, stress, and fear center of the brain, an overactive amygdala can create many problems, including the initiation of a "fight or flight" response. The good news is that a synchronized brain structurally transforms to respond differently to stress. As mentioned before, synchronization of the brain is exactly what happens when you chant daimoku.

Research shows that synchronizing the two hemispheres of your brain shrinks the amygdala. Every time you enter into a whole-brain state, your amygdala shrinks afterwards and the functional connections between the amygdala and the pre-frontal cortex are weakened. This allows you to be less emotionally reactive. Furthermore, your attention span increases and you can be more focused and concentrated on what you are doing right now.

Relax your monkey mind

The whole-brain state has been associated with the decreased activation of our default mode network, which is also sometimes referred to as our wandering "monkey mind". This Buddhist concept refers to when your mind is directionless, going from thought to thought, like monkeys jumping from one tree to the other, chattering endlessly.

A monkey being busy even in a hot spring bath

Are you worried that your partner might get ill, then the next second wondering what to cook for dinner tonight? Then do you suddenly realize that you forgot to do your tax declaration? You are going from one thought to the other.

We all have monkey minds. Fear is an especially loud monkey, ringing the alarm incessantly, pointing out all the things that could go wrong. Entering into a whole-brain state with the help of **daimoku** calms down your monkey mind and tames the monkeys.

Itai dōshin, or, to be in harmony with yourself

Let's look again at what happens when your brain is more coherent. The benefits that arise when both brain hemispheres work together harmoniously consist of an improved and higher focus, more creativity, optimal mental health, improved memory, and the ability to think clearly and make better decisions.

At the same time, your emotions also change as soon as you are in a coherent brainwave state. You feel much happier and more optimistic, as if you are "one with the world". Financial and professional success comes more naturally. I myself have experienced it very often that this condition helped me get my thoughts, feelings and actions into harmony again.

Nichiren called this aspect *itai dōshin* which means "different bodies but one mind". The terms "different bodies" and "one mind" can mean harmony and alignment to the same goals or the same mental attitude in a group of different people.

The "different bodies", however, can also stand for the individual aspects of a human being, such as his or her perception, consciousness, thoughts, feelings or actions. If all these aspects are in itai dōshin then they are in harmony. Do you remember? These are the aspects that make up coherence. Are you in harmony with yourself? When the two halves of your brain produce different brainwave patterns, you are definitely not in harmony with yourself. **Daimoku** gets the two hemispheres of your brain back into itai dōshin.

Dōtai ishin is an incoherent state

The opposite state is described by Nichiren as *dōtai ishin*, which means "one body but different mind".

In this case, the term "one body" may also refer to a group of people who on the outside represent a community but who are not really in harmony with each other. This may result in the group not having a common goal or orientation.

Again, this principle may also stand for the individual aspects of a person, such as his or her thoughts, feelings or actions. If these are not coordinated and in harmony with each another, then you are torn inside. You are in a state of incoherence.

If, for example, you want to be healthy, but you constantly feel the emotion of anger, eat bad food and smoke cigarettes, then what you feel and do does not correspond to your goal. When you want to change your financial karma and reach a stable and solid financial situation, but you constantly feel lack and fear of being poor, then what you feel does not correspond to your future goal. You are in an incoherent state. When you move in with your new partner, but secretly doubt whether it was the right decision, your feelings and your thoughts do not comply with your decision and your actions.

At some point, however, your incoherent state becomes apparent in your external situation. If you remain in a job that is not really fun and gets you down, then your feelings do not correspond to what you are doing. Only when your thoughts, your feelings and your actions coincide can you be successful in what you are doing.

**Nichiren recognized that
coherence was a prerequisite for success.**

Nichiren evaluated the aspect of "many in body, one in mind" (*itai dōshin*) as crucial in order to be successful. He took a very clear stance on this topic and illustrated that even a small army can win over a big army, if there is unity and harmony among them, i.e. if they are in itai dōshin:

If the spirit of many in body but one in mind prevails among the people then they will achieve all their goals, whereas if they are one in body but different in mind then they can achieve nothing remarkable.

The more than three thousand volumes of Confucian and Taoist literature are filled with examples. King Chou of Yin led seven hundred thousand soldiers into battle against King Wu of Chou and his eight hundred men. Yet King Chou's army lost because of disunity while King Wu's men defeated him because of perfect unity.

Even an individual at cross purposes with himself is certain to end in failure. Yet a hundred or even a thousand people can definitely attain their goal if they are of one mind.

Though numerous, the Japanese will find it difficult to accomplish anything, because they are divided in spirit. In contrast, although Nichiren and his followers are few, because they are different in body, but united in mind, they will definitely accomplish their great mission of widely propagating the Lotus Sutra. Though evils may be numerous, they cannot prevail over a single great truth, just as many raging fires are quenched by a single shower of rain. This principle also holds true with Nichiren and his followers. *Many in Body, One in Mind (1279)*

Chapter 7

Consciousness is multi-dimensional

> A human being is part of the whole that we call the Universe. It experiences itself, its thoughts and feelings, as something separate from everything else – a sort of optical illusion of its consciousness.
> – Albert Einstein
>
> World is a multi-dimensional reality. At lower levels, it is full with unconsciousness and competitiveness. At higher level, it is full of beauty, bliss and divinity. Focus on higher dimensions.
> – Amit Ray

Is consciousness a product of the brain?

For a very long time modern science and especially biology has held the view that consciousness in the sense of being aware of oneself is a product exclusively of the brain. It was and is still believed that all emotions and thoughts, any kind of perception and memory, can be reduced to interactions of neurons and biological processes in the brain. In this case, consciousness itself is only driven by chemical and neurological processes and your mind is isolated from your body. As a consequence, you are isolated from your environment. According to this materialistic view, brain death naturally represents the end of one´s consciousness.

At the frontier of science, however, some researchers are challenging this materialist view and have begun to develop a new understanding of the nature of consciousness itself. Sure, we can perceive things around us and ourselves, but what really is consciousness? These scientists don´t think that consciousness is a product solely of our brains. This is like saying that music is the product of a radio.

As it happened, this is exactly what I presumed when I was a child. I thought there were small people in our radio making music. I remember asking my father why these people were so small. I couldn´t figure out how they fit into such a tiny object. However, I remember desperately looking for an explanation for the music that came out of the radio. I wondered what happened to the people when the radio was broken. Only later did I understand that the music continued to exist even after our radio was gone. This is more or less the same question that these new researchers are asking themselves. What actually happens once the brain doesn´t function anymore?

Beyond your brain

In our book NB 3.0 we pointed out that the spiritual dimension beyond time and space presents one of the important implications of the "Ceremony in the Air", as depicted in the Gohonzon. In order to describe this spiritual sphere, we introduced Anita Moorjani´s near-death experience, which she described in a very systematic and clear manner. In recent years, some scientists have tried to investigate near-death experiences in order to illustrate the limitless, endless and universal character of consciousness.

Among those scientists is Dr. Pim van Lommel, who worked as a cardiologist in a Dutch hospital and who became interested in near-death experiences. He compiled the many intriguing stories of his patients who had each survived complete cardiac arrest. The results of his studies suggest that our consciousness exists independently from our body. He argues that if consciousness was a product of the brain alone then this would imply that brain death would stop the activity of consciousness. However, this is not the case. As he reports, people had a very expanded, bright and clear consciousness even under critical condition, in which their hearts and breathing activity had stopped and no more brain stem activity was registered. That´s why many researchers ask themselves:

Is consciousness an intrinsic property of the universe and of reality that has always been there in its non-local form?

Van Lommel reckons that consciousness is endless, timeless and limitless in a spiritual dimension beyond the physical dimension of time and space. This aspect of consciousness is "non-local" in contrast to the "local" everyday consciousness that we experience when we are awake. We are usually only familiar with our local aspect of consciousness. We know "who we are". Our identity normally depends on this local consciousness that encompasses our body, the various roles that we play in life, our work, our possessions, our belief systems, and our personalities. However, this is only one part of reality.

> Are you open to the idea that your local consciousness in the sense of your everyday ego is only one aspect of a non-local, endless and limitless consciousness?

A journey to non-local consciousness

One of those scientists who vehemently claimed that consciousness is solely restricted to our brain is Dr. Eben Alexander. As a renowned Harvard-trained neurosurgeon he spent over three decades working in hospitals and defending his materialist scientific worldview. He thought that he knew exactly how the brain and mind worked until one morning he woke up with a terrible headache. The following seven days completely changed his life and his worldview. What had happened? His brain was severely damaged by a devastating case of bacterial meningitis and he fell into a weeklong coma. It was almost certain that he would die. The medical doctor who was treating him testified a "mortality of 97%".

He was in intensive care and his neocortex did not react any more. From a medical point of view, it was not possible for him to think or to perceive anything, or even to hallucinate in this state.

Yet, Eben plunged into the deepest dimensions of consciousness where time and space did not matter. Most of all he vividly experienced a beautiful world full of light and unconditional love. On top of that, he received one clear message:

> You are always being loved and appreciated; you don't have to fear anything; you can't do anything wrong. – Eben Alexander

On the seventh day of his coma he opened his eyes and unexpectedly started to come back into this life without any brain damage. This was really surprising, for the "best case scenario" from a medical point of view had been that his brain would be damaged forever should he ever wake up from his coma. This near-death experience changed everything that he knew about the brain, the mind and consciousness. He had tapped into non-local consciousness, which caused him to embrace a radically new worldview. Since then he has been sharing his insights into what he considers the true nature of consciousness. He asserts that science can and will determine that consciousness is not restricted to your brain alone and that consciousness survives physical death. He now claims that once you are able to tap into your "greater mind" you can achieve healing, enhance your relationships and receive guidance. He firmly believes that accessing this infinite source of wisdom will ultimately enrich every facet of your life.

According to Eben, consciousness exists entirely independent of the brain. The true nature of consciousness is non-local and much more fascinating than we humans can imagine.
Tapping into this infinite source enables you to improve every aspect of your life.

Scientists like van Lommel also presume that consciousness is not limited to the brain alone, but rather that the brain acts as a kind of receiver and transmitter of consciousness. This could be compared with the different stations you can receive via radio or television. Somehow we are like a kind of individual radio receiver who can tap into this field of consciousness or connect to it. Such a program simply corresponds to the state of life you are in. The frequency of this program also depends on the prevalent frequency of your brainwaves.

> The question is:
> Which state of life are you tuned into at the moment?

It's like watching TV. If you want to watch a program that is on the romance channel and you tune in to CNN, then you will see all kinds of problems, even though you do have the capacity to tune in to a frequency on which the romance channel is broadcasting. But you won't see the romance channel on a frequency called CNN, because it's focused on the problems of the world. This would be a complete vibrational misalignment. It's the same with our awareness, our visions and our intentions. We have to change the vibration that we're tuned into if we want to have different results in life.

What program are you tuned into?

Your Buddha nature corresponds to non-local consciousness

Current researchers tend to believe that consciousness is everywhere and that every animal, stone and plant has consciousness, too. Furthermore, there is actually no individual consciousness at all. We are all embedded in what you might call universal consciousness, an overall, unified field of consciousness. Just as two of the world's leading experts on neuroscience and consciousness, Christof Koch and Giulio Tononi, put it in their profound statement:

> "Consciousness is an intrinsic, fundamental property of reality."

They believe that consciousness is everywhere and that every animal, stone and plant has consciousness, too. We are all embedded in what you might call universal consciousness. "The heart of consciousness is that it feels something and that we have to reduce the suffering of all sentient beings", says Christof Koch.

What is really fascinating, however, is that these innovative theories about consciousness and its multi-layered structure actually correspond to the Buddhist doctrines regarding life, karma and consciousness. Nichiren adopted the idea of Mia-lo (Zhanran, 711-782, the sixth patriarch of the Tiantai school of Chinese Buddhism) that consciousness is everywhere and not restricted to human beings alone. In his gosho *The Object of Devotion for Observing the Mind* he talks about that even stones and plants have enlightened consciousness and therefore even the piece of paper on which the Gohonzon is inscribed contains the state of Buddhahood.

> Miao-lo states in his work "The Diamond Scalpel": "A plant, a tree, a pebble, a speck of dust—each has the Buddha nature, and each is endowed with cause and effect and with the function to manifest and the wisdom to realize its Buddha nature."
> *The Object of Devotion for Observing the Mind (1273)*

This short text illustrates a very important aspect of the Nichiren Buddhist doctrine about life and karma. It tells us that consciousness is everywhere. Furthermore, even things, animals and plants have their own "karma" and are subject to the "law of cause and effect".

For many years people have been asking us: What exactly is my "Buddha nature"? Of course I could initially understand this concept theoretically, but I must admit that I did not embrace it emotionally. In our Western culture there isn't really a term I could relate this abstract concept of Buddha nature to. This changed completely, however, when I learned about new scientific research about the "unified field of energy and consciousness" and the "non-local aspect of consciousness".

I understood that our Buddha nature actually corresponds to this non-local aspect of consciousness in the form of "cosmic consciousness". Nichiren considered this the matrix of all beings and of all phenomena on Earth and in the entire universe. This is exactly what the latest research at the frontier of science suggests: This all-encompassing energy field is considered to be the source of all manifestations and of consciousness itself.

There is an increasing recognition that we are immersed in an overall interpenetrating energy field that is often just called "the Field" or the "Zero-Point-Field". American journalist and author Lynne McTaggert has given a detailed overview of the latest research on this matter.

These new theories suggest that at our most fundamental level we are packets of pulsating energy interacting and exchanging information with this sea of energy. We are never separated from this field from which springs all manifestation. This pulsating energy field is the central engine of our being and our consciousness.

> To be able to connect with this field finally determines how happy or healthy we are.

Karma creates your individual way of life

The above cited text further mentions "the law of cause and effect" that everybody and everything is subject to. Though this aspect relates specifically to the cause for realizing one's Buddha nature, it can also be understood in a more general way in the sense that we are permanently living according to "the law of cause and effect." That is to say that we are always living under the influence of our karma, which we create every moment. That's why each one of us has his or her unique experiences in life. Most surprisingly, this is also what new scientific research suggests:

> We are all part of the same consciousness.
> In this field of consciousness, however, there is
> a wide variety of information and content.

Therefore, what you are experiencing corresponds, so to speak, to the program that you are currently receiving. The frequency of this program depends on your karmic memories, tendencies and causes. It is your individual memory and the collective memory of your family and your country that heavily influences the program you receive.

And this is exactly what van Lommel's patients reported after being resuscitated. Everything that you have ever experienced, done, thought and felt, how you reacted to situations and your predominant feelings: it is all still there on this non-local level of your consciousness. Our thoughts, memories and sensations are all objects of consciousness.

The light behind it all

According to van Lommel, you could compare the ability to experience consciousness with the light of a film projector. The projector sends light to a screen, where the projected pictures are constantly changing. These pictures are your perceptions, emotions, memories, dreams, thoughts and sensations. The film you are experiencing on the screen could be compared to your individual karma. This is the content of your consciousness colored by the effects of everything you have ever experienced, done, thought and felt. It is always there, stored on a non-local level of your consciousness.

Without the light of the projector, however, there would be no pictures.

> If you want to change the projected movie, you definitely have to change the film in the projector.

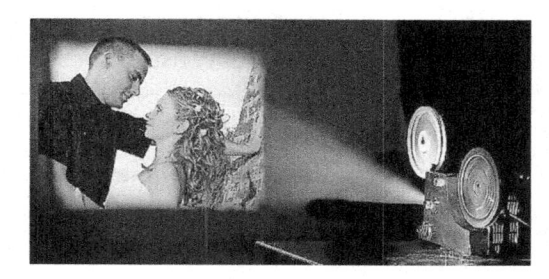

That's not what most of us tend to do, however. Instead we desperately try to change things exclusively on the outside. That would be like shouting at the actors portrayed on the screen to try to make them behave in a different way. Therefore it is really important to change your karma if you want to watch a different film on the screen of your life. Of course, this is easier said than done.

That's why the practice of **daimoku** is not only about realizing your wishes, although that is a fascinating part of it. Nichiren goes one step further and gives us the means to actually change our karma in the depths of our life. How is this possible? In order to change one's karma we need access to a karma-free zone, so to speak. Nichiren gives us the key to this in the above cited Gosho, in which he says that "everything is endowed with the function to manifest and the wisdom to realize its Buddha nature."

Being able to practice the dharma of the mystic law, i.e. the mantra of **Nam-myō-hō-ren-ge-kyō**, enables us to have access to the non-local aspect of our consciousness. By doing so we get the "wisdom" to activate and unfold cosmic consciousness within ourselves in order to realize our visions.

If we don't change our karma, though, we might fulfill our visions but still have the same old unhappy "film" playing in our lives. You might get a new partner, but still have the same old problems. Then you might get a new job, but you still have an obnoxious boss or bullying colleagues. We need access to cosmic consciousness in order to reset our lives. This is why we need an altered and expanded state of consciousness. Our local, everyday consciousness is very limited. Meditation research has shown that access to an altered state of non-local consciousness can be achieved by the state of theta and delta brainwave coherence, as we described in the previous chapter.

On top of that, it is utterly important to work on your negative karmic tendencies, because they always try to sabotage the realization of your dreams. How do you know that you have negative karmic tendencies? You definitely know when you suffer, because these tendencies are often the cause of your suffering or your being unhappy.

Let´s see what Nichiren has to say about the different dimensions and levels of consciousness, how karma works and why changing your karma is one of the key elements of his theory of the nine levels of consciousness.

Chapter 8
The Buddhist deep psychology of karma

> The power of the subconscious is about a million times greater than our conscious mind. — Bruce Lipton

You think you decide consciously

It is very natural to think that we consciously experience our lives and that we consciously make all our decisions using free will. The fact that your conscious self perceives everything in your environment with your sense organs makes you believe that this conscious self is your "I", which doesn't only perceive things but also decides what it is that "you" want to do.

You see the nice flowers in your garden, you hear your children crying, you taste your pizza at the Italian restaurant, you feel your partner's hug on your skin and you smell the flavor of lemon coming from your oil lamp. Your conscious self perceives and processes all this information and tries to make sense of it by comparing everything you see, hear, taste, feel, smell and touch with all the experiences that you have had in the past. Therefore you are much more than your conscious self, for the subconscious mind permanently stores everything that we have ever experienced in our lives: every emotion, every experience, every action and every thought that we once thought. All this, from our childhood up to now. Everything we forget or repress on the conscious level is stored in the subconscious. Any unpleasant event, any hurtful feeling or trauma that was too painful to be processed on the conscious level because it would have overwhelmed us, is stored in the subconscious. Innumerous other experiences and actions are also stored in the subconscious where they are waiting to come up and be finally processed by the conscious mind. Thus, whatever we perceive on a conscious level is only a tiny part of all the possible realities around us.

We now know that the brain processes 400 billion bits of information per second, but consciously we only perceive 2,000 bits per second. These 2,000 bits refer exclusively to what is important in the outer world for survival: Your environment, your body and the perception of time.

Your brain receives millions of messages throughout the day that are being stored in your subconscious, which tries to match these messages by comparing them with memories and emotions stored in your brain. Therefore you experience and interpret whatever is happening to you now according to whatever you experienced in your past, because your brain is basically a record of your past. That's why we often unconsciously tend to perceive that part of reality that "matches" our past experiences.

However, you still think that you make your decisions on a conscious level. Isn't it true that you consciously decide what to wear, what to eat and which car to buy next? You decide which person to start a friendship with and you decide which person that you are going to marry. You feel, of course, that all these decisions are based on your own conscious reasoning and your free will. The latest research, however, strongly contradicts that idea.

An experiment carried out by scientists at the Max Planck Institute for Human Cognitive and Brain Sciences in Berlin revealed that it is not our conscious self that decides what we do, but that it is actually our subconscious mind that decides everything we do seconds *before* we even become aware of it.

In the experiment, participants could freely decide if they wanted to press a button with their right or left hand.

The only thing they had to do was to remember when they made the decision to either use their right hand or left hand.

The researchers would scan the brains of the participants while all of this was going on in order to find out if they could in fact predict which hand the participants would use *before* the participants were consciously aware of the decision. The astonishing result was that by monitoring the participants' brain activity, the researchers could predict which hand the participant would choose seven seconds before the participant was aware of the decision.

> This actually means that you are influenced much more by your subconscious mind than you would have probably thought.

When I read this, I found it quite spooky that decisions are made by my subconscious mind seven seconds before my conscious mind becomes aware of them. However, suddenly I understood on an even deeper level why it is actually very difficult to just "decide" to act and behave differently from now on. It became clear to me that we really have to find the solution to our problems on a deeper level. Once again I realized what great luck it is to have a means to clean my subconscious mind: chanting **daimoku** to the Gohonzon.

Your subconscious mind controls everything

In recent decades, researchers have come to a completely new understanding of how our minds affect the way we live. Scientists are becoming increasingly convinced that how we experience the world, how we perceive things, how we behave and even what decisions we take are largely driven and influenced by the subconscious processes of our mind, and not so much by our conscious mind as we always believed it is. We are constantly influenced by factors that we are not aware of.

What is really surprising is the extent to which we are influenced by our subconscious minds. The mind is always active and independent. It not only plays a critical role in shaping the way our conscious minds experience the world around us, but most of all how we respond to it. Our subconscious mind is our reactive mind. It causes us to react in a certain way.

> The subconscious mind controls 95 percent of how our circumstances manifest and our beliefs shape our lives.

As we shall see later on, this is exactly what Buddhist philosophy already stated more than 1,500 years ago.

We are looking for solutions on the outside

Since our conscious self perceives the world through our five senses, we tend to think that we only have to consciously change something outside of us in order to change our reality. Aren't we always identifying exclusively with what we perceive and represent in the external world? Isn't that where we are always looking for the solution to our problems? Do we not primarily identify with our jobs, what we do or with what we have? Aren't we constantly comparing ourselves to others in terms of our social status, how much we have achieved, how attractive we are, how happy we are and how much money we have? This is your conscious mind, or your ego consciousness, in action.

Therefore we are constantly worried about our life situation and circumstances. On the other hand, we feel some impulses coming up from the deep layers of our minds that we cannot control. These are the familiar feelings that mainly come up when we are by ourselves. That's the part we often want to hide from others. But whenever there is no more distraction from outside, the feelings of anger and helplessness over missed dreams and failed relationships come up. Fear of the future or of your own death cannot be pushed away anymore. The old feelings of worthlessness and self-doubt are there.

Wouldn't it have been better to take up a different profession? My father never supported and appreciated me. What have I really achieved? If only I had taken up the opportunity I was once offered then I would certainly be more successful today! Why is everybody always having more support than I do? Am I not worth it? What shall I do when I am completely alone? I have not managed to be a role model for my children. My children have distanced themselves from me. Such thoughts and emotions break out, especially when your identity is "breaking down" on the outside. When you are losing your job, your children are leaving the house, when you are having problems in your marriage, many questions arise. What is the meaning of my life? What is real happiness? How can I transform these deep-seated emotions?

Most of the time, however, we just keep ourselves busy with various activities in order to escape from the inner stress of the emotions coming up from deep down.

> Our mind is seeking solutions mostly
> in other things, places or people.

Your ego-identity is defined by external stimuli

In my surroundings I have noticed that at a certain point in life people try to escape their upcoming emotions by working really hard. Some just buy a new, fast car. Others just go on a long vacation or undergo beauty surgery. Some are frenetically looking for a new partner on the Internet with whom everything will be better. Others are desperately clinging to the identity of their religious or political community or their football club. Many people spend all their money on expensive restaurants or clothes that make them more and more addictive.

Every evening you might spend hours on Facebook, which makes you feel that you have good friends and that you are important. Maybe you buy one new technical device after the other. Maybe you just eat too much or you go jogging every day.

All these external stimuli distract us in the short term from our true feelings. But the more we consume and as soon as the novelty has gone, we are always stuck in the same identity with the same old feelings. We need more and more external stimuli in order not to feel our emerging emotions.

> In everyday consciousness our attention is directed to the outside world to escape from our feelings of lack and unhappiness.

In this busy state, the mind is usually very restless and has the tendency to lose itself in the external environment. However, it is very difficult to take our attention away from all these things of the outer world, because there are, after all, real problems and threats that we need to focus on. Your children are in puberty, your boss demands certain sales figures, your father is in hospital, the bank demands repayment of your mortgage, lately you are sleeping badly and you often have headaches. You are tired and drained.

> When we are under stress, we define reality through our senses.

In our everyday life we are constantly making decisions, for instance when we are shopping or driving a car. That´s why we firmly believe that only our conscious self, the "thinking ego" of our everyday consciousness, is capable of changing our uncertain position. We believe that we just have to think and act positively and then everything will change. We think we just have to decide to take another direction and then everything will be fine.

But how can we achieve some real change in our situations, if all of our efforts haven´t worked yet? The present situation is precisely the result of all the decisions we have made so far. If we continue to think and feel as we did before, our future will look just the same as it is now.

For the time being it is enough to know that we have to go beyond the boundaries of what we sense outwardly in order to find answers. Your conscious mind is defined by your five senses. This is your ego that consciously considers itself to be separate from everything and everybody else. However, you are so much more than what you can see, feel, hear, touch or taste. There is infinitely much more beyond your physical senses.

Sometimes you may experience specific thoughts and feelings that suddenly arise from deep within. Certain memories may suddenly make you angry, happy or sad. I remember quite vividly the time when I was strolling down the main shopping road in my hometown and suddenly I saw a street musician playing a trumpet. I immediately started crying because he was playing a song that my father used to play on his trumpet. This feeling soared up from somewhere deep within and I could not control it. Certain feelings that come from deep within may make you suffer or even cause you to even finally become ill. Obviously, there are different layers of consciousness that seem to determine what we think, feel, how we react, what we decide and even what we do. And this is exactly what Nichiren stated in his theory of the nine levels of consciousness.

A Buddhist multilayer model of consciousness

Nichiren must have been quite aware about these various aspects and levels of consciousness. He was familiar with the doctrine of the nine levels of consciousness that describes the complex multidimensional reality of human life and of human experience.

The theory of the nine levels of consciousness is based on the teachings of the Tiantai school, which added the ninth level of consciousness to the previously existing theory of eight levels.

This Buddhist "deep psychology" – an approach toward therapy that explores the subtle, unconscious, and transpersonal aspects of human experience – differentiates between the levels of the subconscious. It originally goes back to a Buddhist school called Yogachara which existed from the 4th century AD onwards. These Buddhists practiced yoga and meditation and summarized their experiences and insights into a systematic deep psychology more than 1,600 years ago, long before Sigmund Freud (1856-1939) and Carl Gustav Jung (1875-1961) started talking about "the subconscious."

This Buddhist approach established a multilayer classification of the various forms of perception through our five senses that is organized by the cognitive function of our self-awareness. Within this theoretical framework, the term "consciousness" (skr. vijñāna) actually means the function by which we distinguish between the different forms of perception. You cannot see a melody with your eyes, for example, nor touch it with your fingers. You can only enjoy music with your ears. Thus, each of your five sense organs transmits some specific information about the object of perception that is different from the other forms of perception. Furthermore, these different forms of perception are under the strong influence of your learned notions that serve as a filter for recognizing all incoming information.

In a similar way, the Yogachara school explained that the reality you perceive only exists in your own mind, because whatever you experience is nothing but a projection of your mind. This is to say that everything you perceive is an interplay of the different levels of your consciousness.

Whatever you experience is nothing but a projection of your mind

---

According to the traditional view in Nichiren Buddhism there are nine different levels of consciousness, which are classified as follows:

❶ Seeing
❷ Hearing
❸ Smelling
❹ Tasting
❺ Touching
❻ Thinking mind & ego consciousness
❼ Manas
❽ Alaya and
❾ Amala subconscious.

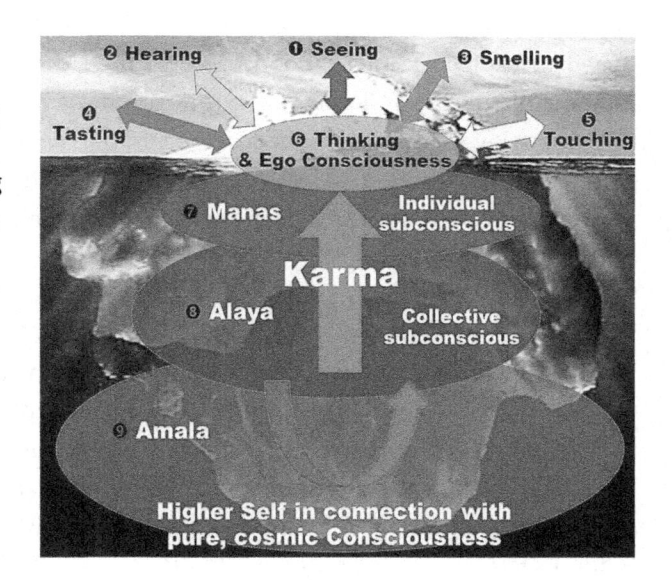

Diagram: Karma model showing senses (Seeing, Hearing, Smelling, Tasting, Touching) above the surface, with Thinking & Ego Consciousness, Manas (Individual subconscious), Alaya (Collective subconscious), and Amala (Higher Self in connection with pure, cosmic Consciousness) below.

According to this deep psychological model, our consciousness can be basically understood to consist of three layers: 1. The "conscious" part of our consciousness (1, 2, 3, 4, 5 and 6); 2. A preconscious state (7); and 3. The subconscious (7, 8 and 9).

The preconscious state is supposed to recall certain memories that can very easily become conscious, whereas it is very difficult to clearly distinguish between the individual (7) and the collective subconscious (8). That´s because they constantly influence each other directly.

You are controlled by your karmic patterns

Your thinking mind actually serves as your "self-awareness" (6) which integrates all the information that you get from your five senses (1, 2, 3, 4, and 5) in order to attribute meaning to what you perceive. This self-awareness means being aware of your "self" or your "ego", knowing that you are you and that you are different from everybody else and the outer world.

This self-awareness in the form of your ego is, however, considered to be just a construction of your mind that is constantly influenced and controlled by the strong impulses coming up from the deep levels of your subconscious mind, which are called "manas" (7). This area of your preconscious mind serves as an interface between your self-awareness (6) and your subconscious (8 and 9).

At the same time this preconscious state at the 7th level also makes up your individual subconscious, which doesn't stop working even when you are deeply asleep or in a coma. You cannot control what you dream when you are asleep. Your dreams will follow their own paths and your conscious ego cannot influence them. Sometimes when you remember what you have been dreaming you are surprised, because dreams can reveal hidden secrets or be a crazy combination of all kinds of information that you have stored deep down in your subconscious.

What beliefs are running your life?

When talking about "karma" we refer to a series of specific patterns about how you think, feel, intend to do things, act and react. At the same time we are dealing with the individual beliefs that have been stored deeply in your subconscious that function as an internal "camera" through which you filter and perceive your experiences on the outside. This camera focuses on any experience on the outside that corresponds to its setting. This means that how you perceive a situation may have little to do with the situation itself, but how you interpret the situation according to your own beliefs that are accompanied by certain emotions.

When we are born, we are wide open and virtually unlimited in the number of possibilities that we can create. I remember quite vividly that when I was a little child I fully expressed myself wildly and without fear. I thought that I could do and become anything that I wanted. The older I got, however, the more I learned that certain behaviors and developed certain beliefs that I took on from my parents, teachers, peers, siblings, relatives and other people around me.

Do you remember the *theta brainwave* we discussed in Chapter 6? When you are a little child before that age of about seven your brain is predominantly in the state of theta. That's when your brain is like a sponge, absorbing everything that other people tell you, and is why at this age you learn things so effortlessly. You formed strong beliefs about your self-image, about money and your role in life, which are now deeply engrained in your subconscious mind.

As a young girl I was often praised for being modest. That made me feel that I had better not become too successful or shine my light too brightly, because then others would envy and reject me. Somehow it made me believe that it was not safe to honestly express how I felt. My mother was constantly on the lookout for what others thought about her and our family, thus giving me the impression that it is far more important what others thought about me than what I thought of myself. My brother lived up to the idea that there is only a limited amount of attention and love going around, so he thought that he had to fight for his share by being mean and obnoxious. To be free from all these limiting circumstances, I really enjoyed going to school and learning something new and exciting every day.

My teachers made me believe that I was very talented and something special. Moving to another town when I was almost six years old, however, made me develop the belief that somehow I don't belong anywhere. When I started school, I was the only girl who did not speak the dialect of the region where we had moved to and who was not exclusively interested in the local events of this small village. I believed that I don't fit in. This mindset influenced my relationships with others for a long time. Only when I started chanting did I realize that this was not true and that it was me who often did not want to fit into the preset mind patterns of certain groups.

I think that was the point that I stopped being so wild and free any more. I lost the feeling that anything was possible and that life was wide open and limitless. The older I got, the more I had the experience that life was full of restrictions and limitations. Other beliefs had taken over. There were good beliefs and negative beliefs.

My father used to tell me that I could succeed in any situation if I was really prepared to stand up for myself. My mother told me that I was very brave and did not fear new situations. Those were good beliefs. But there were also hindering beliefs that led me to the false conclusion that somehow I was inadequate. I stopped paying attention to feeling good about myself but started to think that I was responsible for the happiness of those around me. It took me a long time to realize that this was the reason why, later on in life, I often took on too much responsibility for others. And I was often disappointed of the people whom I took care of. I sometimes had to learn it the hard way that often we do not have the power to make someone else happy, but we do have the power to make ourselves happy.

The good news is that you can transform your negative tendencies and start installing new beliefs when you are chanting. Beliefs are the building blocks of our reality. They influence us and affect us in ways that we seldom even recognize. They vibrate within us day and night on a subconscious level, attracting to us the circumstances and situations that we resonate with.

There is no aspect of our lives about which we don´t have a set of beliefs and assumptions. We have them about our earning capacity, about the state of our health, about our opportunities. Your beliefs are like a program on a computer. What will happen is that this program will play over and over again inside you. If you have limiting beliefs then the program will limit you, it will distract you, it will create circumstances and situations in your life that match the images that you have within. Knowing and understanding this incredible power that beliefs play, we begin to be very observant. We become very conscious of what it is that we are believing.

Exercise 11: Are your beliefs serving you?

Do you recognize yourself in some of the following beliefs and attitudes? Do the following formulations sometimes appear in your "internal dialogues"?

Write down some of your own beliefs and then formulate the exact opposite in the right column.

	Old Belief	New Belief
1	I never have enough money	
2	I never have enough time	
3	I do not deserve it	
4	I'm too old	
5	Life is hard and nobody cares about me	
6	I always have to do everything by myself	
7	Women are at a disadvantage	
8	Men are more severe than women	

9	It is difficult to change reality	
10	I am very similar to my parents	
11	I'm just not lucky	
12	I need at least eight hours of sleep per night	
13	I don't lose weight easily	

Daimoku makes you aware of your karmic tendencies

At this point I would like to share a bitter experience about my unwholesome tendency of sometimes having too much of a "helper syndrome". Unwholesome tendencies or actions are called that way not because they are morally bad but because you are suffering. In the first years of my daimoku practice I realized that I had this karmic pattern of thinking and behaving. I often helped out friends and acquaintances who needed help by providing them with advice or even concrete support in order to solve their problems. Sometimes, however, I went too far with my pity. That wasn´t the right thing to do.

Case study 1: The unpleasant effect of my helper syndrome

One day I met a woman who was supposedly tyrannized by her brother. I could understand her suffering very well based on my own painful experience with my brother. I introduced her to daimoku so that she could overcome her situation. Several months later she told me about a difficult court case she was facing and her obligation to pay the lawyer. Because her lawyer

> required a guarantor for the payment, she asked me to sign the document to take responsibility for the payment in case that she could not fulfill her obligation. She kept promising, however, that I did not have to worry about the money. It was just that her lawyer wouldn't defend her without this signature. I helped her and, as you might have suspected by now, she never paid her lawyer, who then charged me the outstanding amount of money that this woman owed to him. She completely let me down. The lawyer took me to court, but she didn't appear. At the end I had to pay €2,000.
>
> That's when I realized that my "helper syndrome" had gone too far. I felt completely exploited. It often happened to me that I fell into the trap of pity and compassion for the wrong people or to the wrong level. Furthermore, I was very disillusioned to find out that often no-one was there for me when I needed emotional support or practical assistance.

The more **daimoku** I chanted, the more I understood my helper syndrome. This tendency was due to the fact that I had often taken over responsibility for my sick mother when I was a child. That's when I developed the belief that it was up to me whether my mother was happy or healthy. It was many years into my **daimoku** practice that I truly realized that I couldn't change my parents' karma, if they were not willing to do so. You can only change their karma by changing your own karma. Once the energetic imprint of the old experience or tendency is released, everybody in this field of ancestors and relatives is freed from this imprint.

Nam-myō-hō-ren-ge-kyō is the mantra of transformation:
the transformation of negative emotions and tendencies
that cause you to suffer into positive qualities of life
that make you happy and healthy.

With **daimoku** I was now able to build up a healthy relationship with myself. I realized that it was my task to change my own karma. I often had the impulse to help others out of a falsely understood sense of compassion, like too much pity, for instance. After a while, once I had developed the new belief that I am responsible for my own life and others are responsible for theirs, I showed less sympathy for other people who tried to justify their status quo by complaining and blaming others. I increasingly saw the "law of cause and effect" in their lives and their responsibility for their respective situations.

> When we take over too much responsibility for the lives of others we often support other people´s selfishness and help them to remain "victims".

Without knowing it, you adopt certain beliefs. Very often, you are not even aware of it. At some point, it is often more a feeling than a conscious thought. It is as if there are certain scripts that are being played out behind the scenes of your conscious awareness, showing themselves as the constant internal conversations you have with yourself. After years of practicing daimoku, I became aware of my beliefs and that I could change them while chanting.

Another example may illustrate that we are always confronted with our own unwholesome tendencies that are trying to stop us from realizing our wishes and goals.

Case study 2: Anna missed the chance of her life

> Sometimes people will tell you that what they want in life isn't important. They think they just have to earn some money to make a living. I remember quite vividly that this was exactly what Anna was telling me in a group meeting.
>
> She used to live in Berlin but was just visiting a friend in Heidelberg. She just happened to take part in one of our daimoku meetings. Afterwards she told us that she felt quite frustrated with her life, because she was occasionally working as a waitress just to make ends meet.

My husband Yukio asked her what it really was that she wanted to do in life. She told us: "To be honest, I want to be a musical singer. I even had some professional training." However, she thought that she had missed out on a musical career and that now it was too late.

Yukio told her to chant intensively for what she really wanted irrespective of the circumstances of her current situation. I remember that she really took his words to heart and started to chant intensively for two hours a day in order to have a career that really satisfied her.

She soon realized that it was still very much her dream to play a role in a musical. However, she no longer had any contacts in the musical business. Being "realistic", the situation looked hopeless.

One evening she and I decided to meet in an Irish pub in Heidelberg. There I happened to meet Jeannie, an English woman who I had known for about 20 years. I met her occasionally every time I took part in activities of the English-speaking community in Heidelberg, but I never really knew what she did for a living.

That night I was really surprised when Anna, Jeannie and I sat down to have a drink and started talking to each other. It turned out that Jeannie was actually responsible for casting the players in the latest musical that was on at the moment, "Beauty and the Beast". Talking to Anna, Jeannie found out that Anna used to sing in musicals and Jeannie said that they were still looking for somebody to play the role of the Beauty. She had the impression that Anna was the ideal candidate for that role. I could hardly believe that this "coincidence" was all happening in front of me. Here was Anna's chance and the occasion that she had been chanting for. Jeannie really meant it and invited Anna to come to an audition, fixing a time and date the following month.

However, Anna called me two months later to explain that she hadn't made it to the audition. After she had returned to Berlin, she had found a new boyfriend. Because he had a lot of prob-

> lems and even became ill, she thought that she couldn't leave him alone for a couple of days.
>
> Was there nobody else who could take care of him just for two or three days? However, that wasn't the real problem. It seemed to be a predominant tendency in her life. She had often missed out on opportunities to improve her own life because she had always found herself in some chaotic relationship that took up all of her time and energy. Deep down she held the belief that it was more important to please others than to do all that she could in order to become happy herself.

This experience showed me two things. Until today I am still impressed by how accurately the chanting had worked. Nobody could have planned this coincidence beforehand. Anna got the opportunity that she was chanting for. But one has to appreciate such an opportunity and respond as best one can.

If your tendency is to pass opportunities by, then this is when you should take action and chant to overcome your old habits and blockages that stop you from fulfilling your desires. You have to change your karmic tendencies in order to really grow. If you don't honor such an opportunity and let your old tendencies pull you back, you might miss a one-time-only chance and stay stuck in your old situation, which might not be so much fun.

There is one more thing that Anna's experience taught me:

It is never too late to get a new chance when you are chanting, even if your logical mind tells you that it is impossible.

By chanting **daimoku** you will get to know what kind of mindset you have internalized as your subconscious belief. At some point you will be challenged to change this.

Exercise 12: What is your negative tendency?

What is your most important vision in life that you are currently chanting for?

_____

Ask yourself: Do I believe it is possible for me to create this?

_____

Listen to the answer that comes up and identify the core beliefs that stop you from creating what you desire.

_____

If your belief is negative, change it to its opposite while chanting.

_____

Chapter 9

Collective karma affecting your life

> Until you make the unconscious conscious, it will direct your life and you will call it fate. — Carl Gustav Jung

The eighth level: The storehouse of your karma

Our karmic tendencies are very complex. Therefore it is difficult to actually draw the line between our individual and our collective karmas, because they can overlap with each other. Theoretically, however, we can clearly distinguish between the two in order to be able to analyze these two different kinds of influences from our subconscious. The current story in your life is derived from your own experiences, but also from your family and your ancestors. It's more than a memory, though: it's an energy imprint. This energy is the catalyst for thoughts and emotions which create how you feel at the moment. This eighth level of your consciousness is your past self that is also the store of past emotions related to previous experiences and they are replayed in the presence. One of the main aspects of chanting daimoku is to cleanse the energetic imprint of those past experiences, the unconscious shadow that blocks the access to pure consciousness, our potential Higher Self.

One of the reasons for a constricted state of awareness and consciousness is stored emotional pain. When we're experiencing emotional blockages, we can't set the cause for the fulfilment of our vision at a higher state of consciousness. Holding onto anger, for example, we feel caught up in thoughts about the past. Anger makes us feel separate and restricts our access to pure consciousness. However, no matter how long we've been stuck in such a constricted state of consciousness, we can begin to let go of old conditioning and experience our true, unbounded self by chanting daimoku.

> As you release your emotional blockages, joy, freedom and abundance will arise naturally.

Living in a state of inner peace will more and more become your natural way of being. It is from this that state you will attract the people, the experiences and the circumstances that you most deeply desire.

It goes without saying that none of us lives completely separate from other people. You belong to a certain biological lineage of ancestors that can even be traced down to the entire history of mankind. You are also embedded in a certain framework of living such as the natural and sociopolitical environment of your country and its specific cultural imprints. Thus, your life is not just limited to your personal physical and mental existence but also exists in a multi-dimensional and multifaceted relationship with your "collective karmas." Sometimes you might have noticed how German or how American or how Japanese you actually are when you encounter foreigners or when you travel in a country with a completely different culture. In certain situations you might even get the impression that you are experiencing your mother's or your grandfather's feelings.

The cultural categories in your mind

As mentioned before, we tend to regard physical reality as something that is "outside of us". This sensory perception, however, does not only take place directly in your sense organs, but with the help of your brain where your individual sensory impressions are filtered and processed. Therefore we only perceive what we have an idea or image or category or concept about in our consciousness. That means that you will not become aware of things only because you see them through your eyes, but because you have an idea about the object or what you intend to see.

These ideas and categories are often very much conditioned by our cultural patterns. In this respect it is reported, for instance, that the Hopi tribe of Native Americans at some point were not able to distinguish between yellow and orange, because there is no word for "orange" in their language. Since they had no category for this color in their mind, they did not perceive it either.

> It is not only your eyes that see, but your brain that identifies and recognizes the corresponding object and interprets the meaning of a certain behavior.

In the same way, your category for being polite might vary tremendously to that of other people, according to the cultural category of "being polite" you were brought up with.

I experienced this difference with my English friend Shirley. When I was studying in London, I invited Shirley and two other English friends for dinner one evening. After Shirley had finished her plate, I asked her whether she wanted more food. She replied, "No thank you, I'm fine." I cleared away her plate to make room for the desert that I'd prepared. Afterwards I noticed that she was acting a bit strange, and I asked her what the matter was. After a while she told me that I should have asked her one or two times more whether she wanted some more food. She confessed that actually she wanted more food but she considered it rather impolite on my side to just take the plate away. As far as I was concerned, I definitely didn't want to force her to have more food if she didn't want to.

Most Germans I asked about this situation, however, considered asking twice or even three times as rather impolite because in this case they would feel like pushing or forcing the other person to have more food. To push someone to do something was considered by most of the Germans very impolite.

This little scenario tells you how different cultural categories and cultural expectations can be. These factors are the main reason for misunderstandings in intercultural communication. It is reported that more than 60% of failures in international business are caused by these intercultural miscommunications.

Exercise 13: What is your cultural conditioning?

You may have noticed that you have internalized specific patterns of thinking, feeling and acting according to the cultural background that you were brought up with.

Have you noticed any significant differences in the way that you perceive and understand things comparing yourself to members of other cultural groups?

_____

_____

Family karma

Your own consciousness is literally something that goes beyond your own mind. This collective subconscious is the driving force that shapes the course of your life by controlling your individual subconscious, comprised of the previously-mentioned manas, as well as your self-awareness. It is called "alaya consciousness" and literally means "the storage house of karma" because that's where all individual and collective information is "stored."

Every unconscious and unobserved intention and the emotional energy of one's own words is stored in this memory consciousness. Every thought, but also every feeling of anger, frustration, insecurity and anxiety is waiting to unfold its disastrous effect. Just as the effects of all positive feelings and impressions of love and confidence, joy and compassion, as well as all uplifting thoughts, words, and actions, are also waiting to bring their fruit to light.

What we often don´t realize, however, is that everything that is stored in this subconscious layer is affecting us now. This very moment is an accumulation of the sum of all the thoughts, feelings, actions and experiences you´ve had throughout your current life and previous lifetimes. It´s all happening now. Everything your mother, father, siblings, friends, teachers, colleagues, bosses, and everyone around you has ever said to you and how they have ever behaved to you throughout your life is occurring inside your deeper subconscious mind like data stored on a computer memory chip. All this left an energetic imprint that still resonates in the presence. To further illustrate the aspect of family karma I would like to share two experiences with you.

Case Study 3: Part of my family karma

> When I went on a trip to the US with my husband in 2001 I was confronted with what is called "family karma" in a very concrete way. Two years earlier, I received a letter from a distant relative. He belonged to that part of my family that had emigrated to the United States a couple of generations ago. Until then there had been no contact between my family and his family. We each owned the same family tree diagram that some family member had created generations ago so that we could trace back our common ancestors over many generations and he had decided to get in touch.
>
> This relative happened to be called Peter, just like my father. Since he also had the same surname, he had exactly the same name as my father did. The shock and the surprise was great when one day I got a letter from a person called Peter Kiliani, because at first I thought this was a letter from my late father. It really hit me like a hammer. The puzzle was solved quickly, however, and Peter and I soon made personal contact.

Peter came to Germany and wanted to get to know the other members of his European family of origin. When my husband and I were flying to the US one year later, we also took the opportunity to meet Peter's family, our American relatives. It was a really interesting phenomenon. We also met Peter's mother and his sister Kate. When we sat together and had dinner one evening, we told each other many different stories from our respective families. Soon it turned out that exactly the same patterns and experiences occurred within the two families.

The same pattern of two siblings splitting up in an unforgiving manner also existed in the American part of the family, just as it did in the German part of the family between my grandfather and his brother. Something had happened between the two that my grandfather would never forgive. He did not even allow his brother to see him on his deathbed. In the US, twin brothers fell out with each other and completely cut off their relationship. From that moment on, there was no more contact between them and their family members.

This phenomenon was probably one aspect of deeply rooted family karma that was obviously active independent of time and space. Above all, Peter and his sister Kate told me that they recognized the pedantic behavior of my German aunt to be prevalent in their mother's behavior, too. We laughed a lot when we realized that we were having exactly the same problems and conflicts within our respective families.

Case Study 4: A deep passion for flamenco

Another experience also made it clear to me that inherited family patterns really do exist. During an SGI training course in Trets in the south of France, I met a woman who, like myself, felt a deep love and passion for flamenco. We sat together one evening and she told me that she had always been attracted to flamenco, even when she was a child. She was originally adopted from South America and she grew up with a loving and caring family in Germany. Years later, she wanted to get to know her biological mother and she managed to actually meet her. That´s when she found out that her mother was a flamenco dancer.

I was very touched by this story because it showed me how preferences, impressions, attitudes and emotions are contained in our family karma or in our DNA given a modern perspective. This might be the attraction to a certain kind of dance, but it might also be the tendency to get angry, to be happy or to be depressed.

Exercise 14: What is your family karma?

What kind of conflict patterns or attitudes can you observe within your family? What reoccurring problematic situations cause you to suffer?

_____

_____

The informational patterns of past generations

These observations show that our family karma seems to be rooted in the deep subconscious of our lives. Therefore you can´t just change it by simply analyzing it, wishing or thinking positively. Your everyday ego cannot get access to the patterns of thinking and feeling stored in your collective subconscious.

This subconscious level contains memories from past lives or deep genetic memories, i.e. programs that are being carried over from ancestors. In the same way that our individual memories are stored in our neural pathways, this kind of collective memory is also stored in our body and our cells. In his book *Intelligent Cells* biologist Bruce Lipton describes how memories and emotions are handed down from generation to generation through our genes.

> Informational patterns of karmic tendencies are handed down through our genes from generation to generation.

Upon reading Bruce Lipton's book, I suddenly understood all the similar experiences and emotions between me and my grandfather, who like me was fascinated by Buddhist philosophy. Did I just have the exact same "informational pattern" as he did? Was I acting out a certain pattern handed down from generations beforehand? Had I just stored the information of my mother's and grandmother's feelings of fear and uncertainty during difficult economic times during the Second World War? Was I just constantly reactivating those patterns? The emotions, core beliefs and programs of your parents and your grandparents might well be added to your genes in this life. According to Lipton, it is these energies that tell your DNA how to behave. I was stunned. Wasn't that exactly what Nichiren had already said more than 740 years ago?

> The greatest evil among evils produces consequences that not only affect the perpetrators personally but extend to their sons, their grandsons, and so on down to the seventh generation. And the same is true of the greatest good among good.
> The Venerable Maudgalyāyana put his faith in the Lotus Sutra, which is the greatest good there is, and thus not only did he himself attain Buddhahood, but his father and mother did so as well. And, amazing as it may seem, all the fathers and mothers of the preceding seven generations and the seven generations that followed, indeed, of countless lifetimes before and after, were able to become Buddhas.

| *On Offerings for Deceased Ancestors (1279)* |

In this letter, Nichiren made it clear that you stay under the influence of all the positive and negative karmic patterns your ancestors have caused in the last seven generations.

At the same time, you are causing respective effects not only for your own life, but also for your descendants in the following seven generations. Therefore, changing your family karma in this life also means changing the karma of future generations.

The energy of daimoku therefore has the power to alter the informational patterns stored at this deep subconscious level in such a way that a positive reality can be experienced. This obviously happens on a spiritual level beyond time and space where everything happens at the same time. This also explains why the past of our ancestors, or the effects of the contents stored in this field of consciousness, can be transformed for all members of a family at the same time.

Therefore there is a deep meaning in praying for the happiness of your beloved ones who have already passed away!

Your karmic tendencies always influence your life

As already explained, Nichiren´s Buddhist deep psychology clearly shows that we live under the permanent influence of our own karma. Our karmic tendencies are both of individual and of collective nature and are stored in the deep subconscious layers of our minds. The reality you experience within yourself and outside of yourself is actually shaped by your own subconscious patterns of thought and behavior.

This means that the karmic patterns stored in your subconscious mind are always dominating and directing your life. Therefore it is an illusion to think that you can change your outer situation without changing your inner disposition first. That´s what most people are trying to do by investing a lot of money, time and energy in trying to change their environment.

> Your environment, however, is always a reflection of your mind.

The reason you are experiencing something you didn´t consciously wish for is that your subconscious programing constantly sends out a certain vibration that pulls similar vibrations into your life.

However, when you chant **daimoku** the change starts immediately in the depth of your subconscious mind and will be reflected in your environment.

> This means that your karmic tendencies attract a specific situation that happens to you and that you enhance by reacting to the situation in a certain way.

The biggest illusion that we constantly fall for, however, is to assume that there are primarily other causes for our own situation than our own state of life and consciousness. This means that we are always confronted with the same topics, tendencies, feelings, thoughts, reaction patterns, beliefs and memories until we change our karmic tendencies. If you constantly compare yourself to others and react in a competitive way instead of seeking to work harmoniously together with other people, for instance, you might have a lot of confrontation in your life. If you constantly react with fear to any new situation or job offer you get, then this might be exactly what stops you from progressing and growing.

This also means that in order to change your life it is necessary to become aware that it is always your own karmic tendencies that prevent you from fulfilling your desires and your visions. These karmic tendencies form the basis of all your activities and experiences and therefore influence all areas of your life, such as your health, success, wealth, family, and relationships with friends and partners.

If you tend to react with fear, for instance, then it will affect all areas in your life. I remember at the beginning of my practice, when I became aware that I was projecting my fear-based pattern onto almost everything, that this was the main challenge I would overcome by practicing daimoku. When fear runs your life, you probably fear asking to be paid more for your work because you fear losing your job. I remember that I used to be very nervous when I started teaching seminars at international companies. I would sleep badly and almost couldn´t breathe before going there. I was stuck in fear and limitation. That´s when I started surrendering my fear to the Gohonzon every time it came up. When I could not chant to a Gohonzon because I was in a seminar, for instance, I would quickly imagine a Gohonzon in front of me and just surrender this feeling to it, knowing that activating the higher power of cosmic consciousness would transform any situation.

You may have the tendency to not finish things or to not really commit to anything. If you tend to go to the gym and only superficially do some of the exercises and tell yourself that next time you will do it properly, then this is very likely how you do everything in your life. This pattern may also show itself in your partnership, because you are not committing to your boyfriend or your family or you are always putting things off.

> How you do you anything is how you do everything.

Even when you chant you can repeat your karmic patterns again and again if you do not really put some effort into becoming aware of them and consciously facing them. I realized after a while that many people tend to react in a very unpleasant or negative way once you tell them the karmic patterns that impair their progress.

Case study 5: An inconsistent way of living

> Chris had already been practicing daimoku for some years but somehow refused to face the very pattern in his life that caused himself and others to suffer. He had the underlying pattern of never finishing things and really taking responsibility for his life or for the people he was responsible for. This pattern showed itself when he did not finish his University studies, although he was very intelligent and talented. He used to do many things but did not get his priorities right. He just could not focus on doing what was really important at the moment. This would have been to finish his final thesis in order to get a University degree. Instead he put his energy in his hobbies, in meeting friends and in playing musical instruments.
>
> One of his friends pointed out to him that it would be better for him to finish his studies and that his tendency of not prioritizing or finishing things disrupted many areas of his life. Chris really didn't like this advice, and was annoyed and sulky for some time.
>
> Later on he had a child with his girlfriend, but he never managed to keep a proper job and to provide a financially-stable situation for his young family, leaving it to his girlfriend. What was really surprising was the fact that soon after they split up he became a father again with his new girlfriend, even though he couldn't financially support the child he already had.

Thus, even when you chant daimoku it is essential that you have a close look at the results in your life in order to become aware of your underlying karmic tendencies. This is the first and often most difficult step towards changing them. When you chant daimoku, however, the situation sometimes becomes so drastic on the outside that you cannot ignore your own underlying tendency any more.

This was illustrated in my own karma-based experiences (See the Case Studies *My helper syndrome* and *My family karma*, Chapter 8). You may have many of your own stories to tell in this respect.

By now you may have realized that your own karma is constantly causing you problems. That's why we are going to take a closer look at the specific mechanisms of karma, i.e. how it actually works.

A fatalistic view of karmic retribution

The word *karma* first of all incorporates *voluntary action in the form of thinking, speaking and acting*. It refers to everything you consciously decide to do. The *law of karma* states that sooner or later every action inevitably causes a certain *effect* that corresponds to the previously set *cause*. We call this the law of cause and effect. Ancient Buddhist texts give some specific examples of this principle:

> One who climbs a high mountain must eventually descend. One who slights another will in turn be despised. One who depreciates those of handsome appearance will be born ugly. One who robs another of food and clothing is sure to fall into the world of hungry spirits. One who mocks a person who observes the precepts and is worthy of respect will be born to an impoverished and lowly family. One who slanders a family that embraces the correct teaching will be born to a family that holds erroneous views. One who laughs at those who cherish the precepts faithfully will be born a commoner and meet with persecution from one's sovereign. This is the *general law of cause and effect*.
>
> Quoted from the Nirvana Sutra in:
> *Letter from Sado (1272)*

In the above-cited passage Nichiren gives some examples for the traditional understanding of the *general law of karma*. Karma is also energy. The energy created by an action has to be returned. It cannot be avoided. This law can be characterized as the *principle of karmic retribution,* which in simple terms means:

> You reap what you have sown.

Thus, you are always confronted with the effects of everything that you have thought, said and done in the past. Since you are not quite aware of all these actions you may sometimes wonder why you are confronted with certain situations that make you suffer.

When you consider this principle of karmic retribution consistently you will come to the conclusion that you definitely should avoid negative emotions, thoughts and actions that harm or destroy yourself and others. Instead you should do your best to respect and treat yourself and others well. Based on this insight, Buddhists were traditionally encouraged to observe hundreds of specific ethical precepts and moral regulations.

In Nichiren Buddhism, however, there is not a long catalogue of dos and don'ts describing a moral code in detail. In contrast, Nichiren offered a completely different approach to changing and overcoming all our karmic tendencies that are the cause of our suffering.

Instead of following various precepts to lead a morally-decent life, Nichiren suggested we should focus on directly activating the enlightened state of life. Later on we will come back to this fundamental difference in the understanding of karma and how to deal with it.

Considering the principle of karmic retribution, everything you experience in the present is therefore predetermined by your own actions in the past. You are just harvesting the fruit that has grown from the seeds you have sown. According to this understanding, it is your karma to meet a certain person or to be involved in a certain event or situation. In this respect, karma is generally understood as something fateful and as something that happens in a deterministic, fatalistic way.

> The fatalist view of karmic retribution makes your life seem predetermined – but are you truly powerless?

Your autopilot mechanism makes you a victim

Neuroscientists have found out that the human brain acts in a very strange way: It barely registers pleasant experiences, but it overemphasizes every little disappointment.

Let´s say that you applied for a job, but someone else got it. If this disappointment makes you think that "I'll never succeed" or "I'm just not smart enough" then your subconscious mind will find a way to attract certain people and situations in the future to prove that you are "right". Remember, your subconscious mind does not distinguish between what is real and what is imagined.

Case study 6: Petra's disappointment

Petra is a very attractive and entertaining woman in her mid-fifties who always had the wish to be involved in a TV show supporting women in their everyday lives. She took up the courage to chant for this life goal and she also developed a strategy to reach her goal. She found a company that helped her to produce a professional video clip in which she presented her idea and introduced herself. She sent this video clip to a certain TV broadcasting company that she had in mind. Unfortunately her application was turned down and she was deeply disappointed. This incident automatically triggered the old feeling of being rejected within her and she was so discouraged that she stopped applying to other TV broadcasting companies. Feeling completely insecure, she considered this negative response to be an omen that she would never be successful.

A few days later she started to chant about the matter and she was able to attribute a different, more resourceful meaning to the whole incident. She realized that she was conditioned to automatically react in a certain way whenever she was rejected.

> The rejection had given her the feeling that her entire personality had been rejected. This was exactly the self-limiting feeling that had always held her back from progressing. After chanting in order to transform the situation, she suddenly felt that her idea was not necessarily what this TV broadcaster was looking for, but might just be perfect for another. Now she was determined to continue applying with other TV companies.

The moment that Petra became aware of her own *autopilot mechanism*, she was confronted with the *situation* that her first application had been rejected. Usually she *reacted* automatically to such a situation in a very pessimistic way, feeling as if her entire personality had been devaluated. As a *result* of her own reaction she was deeply disappointed and scared, and so she stopped ap-

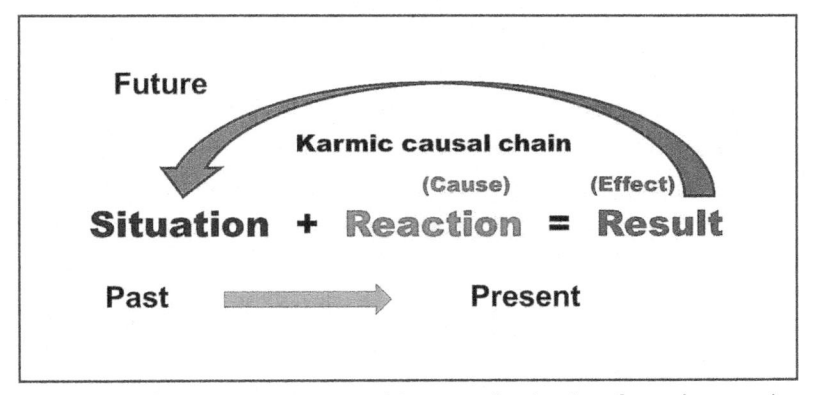

Future

Karmic causal chain

(Cause)   (Effect)

Situation + Reaction = Result

Past ⟹ Present

plying to other companies. In this case she had to face the resulting *new situation* of being depressed. Actually she was in a vicious circle.

A series of *past* actions conditioned your *present* reaction to the situation you are facing right now. The result of this reaction, in turn, determines your reactions in the *future*.

Repeating the same experience again and again

If you aren't given the opportunity to break this causal chain of karma, you are usually forced to repeat the same or similar experiences again and again, further confirming your current mindset and your subconscious beliefs.

Due to this vicious circle, your life situation can even deteriorate over time. You may begin to wonder why you always get into certain negative situations and try to find a logical reason for the serious causes and errors that you might have made in the past. Or you may easily come to the conclusion that somebody else might be responsible for your difficult life situation. That's when you are likely to blame and complain about the person who is supposedly responsible for your situation.

This *fatalistic understanding of karma* arises any time that you view your current and past situations. In this case you may consider the situation that you're in as fateful and unavoidable.

That's when you see yourself as a victim and might think, "I can't do anything about it"; "That's just the way I am"; "They're to blame for my misery"; "I need help from others because I can't manage by myself"; "I feel guilty about what happened. Everything is my fault".

Most people intend to solve this problem by trying to change their outer circumstances. However, your karma is accompanying you all the time. Even if you change your partner, you might get involved in a similar conflict with your new partner. Even if you get more money and a new house, you may just end up having more debts than ever before. Even if you move somewhere else, you might have the same problems that you had before with your new neighbors. Even if you change your job, you might end up with a boss or with colleagues who try to bully you. Even if you get new friends, you'll soon feel let down by them again on an emotional level.

Have you ever experienced something like that? Can you see how persistent your karma can be? Trying to change your outer circumstances alone cannot be the solution to any problem you are facing. It is essential to change the internal karmic pattern in your subconscious mind. That's why sometimes you might feel overwhelmed by trying to find a solution in your outer circumstances, and feel like a victim which may be an excuse for your current situation.

Exercise 15: Victimization

1. Can you think of any situation where you feel that you are repeating the same experience again and again?

   _____

2. Do you notice that in this situation you tend to use one of the above-mentioned phrases said by a victim?

   _____

3. What is going on in your mind whenever you think that way?

   _____

4. What emotions do you feel?

   _____

5. What thoughts do you think?

   _____

6. How do you act in such a situation?

   _____

> It is easy to blame someone else for your difficult situation. In reality, however, you have only given up your own opportunity to change your karma and to develop your innate capacity for transforming this situation.

So far, we have learned that karma begins with your *conditioned patterns of thinking, feeling and acting.*

> To change your karma or a certain karmic causal chain is to change *the way that you react* when you are being confronted with a certain situation.

This requires stopping the autopilot program that drives you directly to a preset direction. However, for most people that is easier said than done. Karma does not exist outside of you; it is deeply engrained even in your body, as we shall see later on.

> Stopping or changing your subconscious autopilot programs can sometimes be difficult to put into practice.
> Therefore you need access to a greater power than the limited state of consciousness of your everyday ego.

Chapter 10

The karma free zone of pure consciousness

> The more you allow your consciousness to expand, the more you will experience a life that is as close as possible to Heaven on Earth.   — Deepak Chopra

The ninth consciousness is within you

According to Nichiren, there is a clear solution to breaking out of this never-ending circle of our patterns of karmic reactions. By inscribing the Gohonzon, he left us a bullet-proof means to break through our karmic restrictions by having direct access to the powerful cosmic consciousness.

In the last two Chapters 8 and 9 we explained the Buddhist deep psychology of karma, consisting of the eight levels of consciousness developed by the Yogachara school. In Nichiren Buddhism, however, we are familiar with the additional level of the ninth consciousness, which is proclaimed in the traditional line of Chinese Tiantai and Japanese Tendai Buddhism. At this point you may ask yourself: Well, why was it essential for Tiantai to assume that underneath the already existing eight levels of consciousness, as taught in the Yogachara school, there was another level of consciousness? What kind of practical benefit can we get from this innovative theory of a Buddhist deep psychology?

First, let's go back to what the Yogachara school taught. The Yogachara school established the view that everything you experience, both inside and outside of yourself, is a direct product and result of your own state of consciousness. This basically means that all our experiences are activities of consciousness. Our thoughts and emotions can heal us or make us sick. It means that your consciousness determines the reality that you experience. When you look at the world "out there," you are really experiencing it "in here," in your consciousness.

Thinking that consciousness precedes the material world goes completely against the Western idea of how reality is structured. We think that the physical universe is "real" and that consciousness is some kind of a by-product of the physical world at most. According to the Yogachara school, however, there is no one indisputable reality. There is only what each of us perceives and then interacts with. They held the view that consciousness comes first, followed by manifestation in the physical world. This applies to your health, your relationships, what you think and how you feel, and what situations you attract.

In order to overcome and change the karmic conditions controlling your life, the Yogachara practitioners made incessant efforts to transform each and every single karmic pattern stored in the eighth layer of their subconscious mind, the alaya-consciousness. It is needless to say that this arduous and tedious practice of cutting off all your karmic influences may take several life times or even eons. The Yogachara practitioners were convinced that at the end of their excruciating effort they would finally reach enlightenment.

Overcoming your self-centeredness

In order to reach this state of Buddhahood, there has always been one big obstacle to overcome: our ego-attachment, which is based on the idea that our conscious self is independent and separate from everything else and is in control of our lives.

The Yogachara school had already asserted that one has to overcome one's tendency toward self-centeredness. Your self-attachment shows itself in various ways, such as when you are overly proud of yourself, or love yourself in a narcissistic way. Since they suggested that everything in your world is created by the projection of your various karmic contents stored in the eighth layer of your subconscious mind, your alaya-consciousness, everything that you are experiencing could be considered a projected illusion.

> If you want to experience a different story on the screen of your life, you have to change the film that is being projected.

Since your conscious self is the center of perception, this illusion could also be regarded a delusion. In this rather extreme way the Yogachara practitioners endeavored to gradually and extensively practice the Bodhisattva way, including meditation to free themselves from all karmic influences and to reach the goal of enlightenment.

Tiantai defined this final goal as the ninth consciousness, also called the "amala-consciousness". This enlightened state of consciousness corresponds to the concept of "buddha nature", which is free from any karmic influence and ego-attachment and presents the matrix of everything in the entire universe.

However, just like the Yogachara school, Tiantai followed the idea that you have to undergo a long, gradual development in order to reach this enlightened state. Even Tiantai didn't expect to finish this task in his present life time.

Thus you can only gradually transform the levels of your karmic tendencies step by step. Let´s suppose every star in the sky would represent one of the numerous aspects of your negative karmic tendencies. Can you imagine how much energy and time you would need in order to eliminate all your negative forms of karma?

> **Exercise 16: What are your karmic tendencies?**
>
> Write down three serious karmic tendencies you are often confronted with in your life. You may describe each of them considering recurring situations, your specific way of reacting to it and the result of your reaction.
>
> 1. _____
>
>   _____
>
> 2. _____
>
>   _____
>
> 3. _____
>
>   _____

Nichiren's Buddhism of the shining sun

This approach of gradual self-development as practiced by the Yogachara school, however, was somewhat too painstaking and troublesome for Nichiren. He wished to establish a much easier method for everyone to overcome their respective karma. Thus, he offered a completely different way of having *direct and instant* access to the enlightened state. He often described the difference between these two types of attaining enlightenment by comparing one's negative karma with the stars in the sky and the state of enlightenment with the sun:

> When the sun rises, the stars go into hiding.
> *The Selection of the Time (1275)*

Imagine that you are gazing at numerous twinkling stars at night and this gigantic scene in heaven represents all the events that have made you suffer in the darkness of illusion and delusion. Now, imagine what happens when the sun rises. Its shining brightness is much more powerful than the twinkling stars. They lose their effect, although they are still there.

Likewise, you don´t have to struggle endlessly to solve your problems for years. That is bound to end in frustration and exhaustion. Instead, you can directly activate the unlimited wisdom and energy of pure consciousness in order to freely design your life at an expanded state of consciousness and to create health and happiness. This is about fulfillment in *every* area of your life, not just in one or two.

All your circumstances will change
as a result of changing your state of consciousness.

Having direct access to this enlightened state of consciousness corresponds to the concept of having access to your inherent Buddha nature. This is your "true self", which is free from any karmic imprints.

> Never seek this Gohonzon outside yourself. The Gohonzon exists only within the mortal flesh of us ordinary people who embrace the Lotus Sutra and chant Nam-myō-hō-ren-ge-kyō. This means the "palace of the ninth consciousness, the unchanging reality that reigns over all of life's functions.
> *The Real Aspect of the Gohonzon (1277)*

The theory of the nine levels of consciousness is concerned
with the core question of our true identity and
the question of the level
at which we can transform our reality and change our karma.

Do you remember the Ceremony in the Air, which represents a spiritual level beyond time and space? In our book *Transform Your Energy – Change Your Life: Nichiren Buddhism 3.0* we described it as a spiritual sphere, an energy field free of matter and duality, not restricted by any constraints of time and space, where all possibilities exist. This is the level of pure consciousness.

> Under the aspect of the Buddhist deep psychology, this area of empty space "in the air" corresponds to the ninth consciousness set forth by Nichiren.

Do you remember Dutch cardiologist Pim van Lommel, who we mentioned in Chapter 7 and who refers to "local" and "non-local" consciousness? "Non-local consciousness" corresponds to what in Nichiren Buddhism is called your "Buddha nature" or the "ninth level of consciousness".

Nichiren considered this the matrix of all beings and of all phenomena on Earth and in the entire universe. This concept might be understood as the equivalent to the source of all manifestations and of consciousness itself. Spiritual traditions tell us that all things come from this source, and there could be even parallels with quantum physics, which deals with the most minute aspects of the physical universe. The greatest physicists and minds of our time suggest that you have infinite potential to create everything you desire within this field. This non-local, non-material field of consciousness is considered to be the source of our mind, our thoughts and emotions. It is often called the field of infinite possibility and is also being referred to as the zero point field. In this realm, which is basically everywhere and nowhere, we are all connected, we are all one.

Nichiren calls this level *"the unchanging reality that reigns over all of life's functions"*. This is the place where healing takes place and where every intention is immediately fulfilled. By inscribing the Gohonzon, Nichiren gave us a means to tap into this field and create results that eventually are reflected in the third dimension of our everyday lives.

> To be able to connect with this field has a great impact on how happy or healthy we are.

You start by activating non-local consciousness

Thus, chanting **daimoku** to the Gohonzon means that your individual personal consciousness is connected to pure consciousness. Whereas pure consciousness is actually unlimited, you as an individual only represent a limited aspect of this unlimited consciousness due to your karmic restrictions, beliefs and your limited self-image. However, by having direct access to pure non-local consciousness you yourself can become unlimited consciousness without any form, and change your karma, your self-image and your entire world. This is the most liberating experience that you can imagine, because it liberates you from the deadlocked idea that you are a limited being restricted by your past and your circumstances.

Nichiren knew to differentiate between the source of pure consciousness and its manifestations that basically consist of the ten different states of life. However, the source of all phenomena is the ninth consciousness which is nothing but pure consciousness.

> Myōho-renge-kyō represents the ninth consciousness, while the Ten Worlds represent the levels from the eighth consciousness on down.
> *The Record of Orally Transmitted Teachings*

Experiencing pure consciousness is actually our true nature, whereas everything we normally identify with is only a filter that is being put on this non-local, formless and unlimited consciousness. Through this filter we only experience our body, our identity, our social surrounding, our possessions and our achievements;

the limited experience of our reality on Earth. We live in a world full of separation, distinguishing between you and I, being a man or a woman, between here and there, between now and then.

Human consciousness is a part of universal consciousness.

The Buddhist psychology shows us that, on the ninth level of consciousness, our mind is not distracted by the perception of external stimuli. We can put our mind in a state where we are fully awake, where there is only clarity, healing and transformation. A state in which our conscious ego can expand and experience the state of pure being. Our fearful thoughts then come to rest. This is the natural state of our mind.

This is like "coming home" for your mind. This is the most pleasant condition in which to be yourself. Whenever I chant, I feel that I really am myself. I am at home. If you really are yourself, then that is a very powerful experience, through which you can bring about profound changes in all aspects of your life.

This cosmic consciousness is defined as a state of complete freedom and happiness. By having access to this level of pure consciousness, karma loses its effect and can no longer bear fruit again.

Exercise 17: Can you imagine...?

Whilst chanting, can you imagine that you are a pure, unlimited, free consciousness that is free of the limitations of your current situation?

Can you imagine that you have released any form of anger and resentment?

Can you imagine that you are free from emotional blockages and unhealthy patterns of behavior?

Can you imagine that there is no limitation on what you can achieve?

Can you imagine that you can always respond at the highest level of consciousness no matter how anyone else behaves?

Can you imagine that your consciousness expands to your free unlimited nature whilst chanting?

Don´t confuse outer reality with the source

We often think that our present circumstances – our jobs, our partners, the money that we have, our friends, our houses, our cars and everything that we have – are the source of our happiness. We tend to do this especially with our respective jobs and our partners. We all know thoughts like this: "if I quit this job, then I won´t have any more income." "if I break up with this person, then I won´t have any more love."

> This is confusing outer reality with the source.

The particular job that you have right now is not the *source* of your abundance. It is a way pure consciousness *unfolds* itself in your life. We often confuse the one person we are in a relationship with as the only source of our happiness. A relationship is the means by which we deliver our love. However, this source is inside of us.

According to Nichiren, the source of our creativity, our happiness and our abundance is pure consciousness. The more we activate it and the more we are connected to it, the happier we are. All of the things that we need and want are being delivered to us by something much bigger than any of us. However, when we get too attached to the individual channels we start to suffer. Our assumptions about the true sources of our happiness are not absolutely true. There are infinite ways to attain abundance, and there are infinite ways to attain happiness. They all come from that one place, which is unmanifested pure consciousness that is unfolding in your life.

"Slander" is to deny the dignity of your life

Nichiren's innovative approach to changing your karma is essentially based on tapping into your Buddha nature, which can be activated immediately by chanting **daimoku**. We identified the Buddha nature inherent in our lives to be identical with the ninth consciousness. This part of your consciousness is pure potentiality. It has no beginning or end, no space or time. It has infinite organizing power and makes quantum leaps of creativity, and it moves naturally in the direction of growth. It's an impersonal self that is also known as universal consciousness, cosmic, non-local and unlimited consciousness, but it finds expression in time and space through a body. It is the only true source in the sense of a continuous self while we are awake and sleep. When chanting **daimoku**, this potential self, the center that allows you to fall back in love with your life, can rise.

Based on this insight Nichiren stresses that everyone is endowed with the potential to realize enlightenment. Translating this Buddhist doctrine into modern terms, what we refer to as Buddha nature or as non-local consciousness actually could be called the "dignity of life." Therefore both **daimoku** itself and the Mandala Gohonzon actually represent the dignity of life, which should be highly respected. That's why every time you chant daimoku towards the Gohonzon, you appreciate the dignity of life and at the same time you express the intention to unfold this potential in your own life.

It is essential to realize that Nichiren didn't think that the "general law of karma" was the basic cause of his suffering, since the general law of karma only describes the cause for each of his innumerous, individual, negative forms of karma. According to Nichiren, there is a much deeper and more profound basic reason for why you are suffering. Once you are able to transform this one basic reason, you do not have to bother to try and change all the 3,000 different forms of your negative karmas. Changing the base cause changes all. In this sense Nichiren stated that the fundamental cause of his own sufferings was caused by slander:

> This is the *general law of cause and effect*. My sufferings, however, are not ascribable to this causal law. In the past I despised the votaries of the Lotus Sutra. I also ridiculed the sutra itself.
> *Letter from Sado (1272)*

If you only consider and follow the general law of karma or the principle of karmic retribution, then you are mainly concerned to overcome each one of your negative karmas that cause you to suffer. As mentioned above, this effort means an endless struggle and will end only in frustration and exhaustion. In Nichiren Buddhism, however, all these karmas are transformed by activating the Dharma of Nam-myō-hō-ren-ge-kyō. Since this Mystic Law contains all kinds of benefits, you don't have to be concerned with the question of how to change and overcome all individual forms of karma that are the cause of all your suffering. Instead your main focus should be to activate the enlightened state of life being filled with unlimited compassion, love, wisdom and happiness. It is the sun that rises to outshine the stars which are your negative forms of karma.

Let's illustrate this principle. Suppose you owe your bank $10,000 and the bank is now demanding that you pay this sum back. This will be a heavy burden on you if you are earning $10 an hour in your current job. If suddenly, however, you get $100,000 from an unexpected source, then paying back the $10,000 is not a big deal and doesn't bother you anymore. The unexpected fortune is like the sun, and the paltry debt of $10,000 are like the stars, no longer worth your worry. You can easily handle that. Now you have an enlarged capacity to handle this demand of your individual karma.

When Nichiren mentioned that his sufferings were caused by his "slander of the Mystic Law" (*Hōbō*), represented by the Lotus Sutra, he related all of his problems and his negative forms of karma to one simple question: are you *pro* or *contra* the Mystic Law? By doing so he emphasized that the most fundamental problem in our life is the slander of the Mystic Law.

The Mystic Law doesn't, however, just mean the law of causality, but life itself, since it embodies and manifests this law. As Nichiren often emphasizes, our life as such is precious and to be respected. Therefore, slandering the Mystic Law can be understood today as any action that denies our valuable life and our potential of realizing the enlightened state of being.

However, whenever we appreciate our life and activate its highest potential we will be put into a position to change all our individual negative forms of karma together.

In modern terms, the "slander of the Mystic Law" can be understood as denying the dignity of our lives and not seeing the potential that we can activate and unfold it in our daily lives.

Ichinen Sanzen represents this basic principle

The possibility of activating the enlightened state of life is also the reason why in Nichiren Buddhism we don't have a long list of dos and don'ts, but only one precept: the "precept of the diamond chalice."

> The five characters of Myōhō-renge-kyō, the heart of the essential teaching of the Lotus Sutra, contain the benefit amassed through the countless practices and meritorious deeds of all Buddhas throughout the three existences. Then, how can these five characters not include the benefits obtained by observing all of the Buddhas' precepts? Once the practitioner embraces this perfectly endowed wonderful precept, he cannot break it, even if he should try. It is therefore called the *precept of the diamond chalice*.
>
> *The Teaching, Practice, and Proof (1274)*

This precept outshines all others. All the above-mentioned aspects are based on the typical way of thinking in Nichiren Buddhism, that you start from one point to solve all problems in your life.

> Whatever has happened to or been done to you in your life, there is always a certain part of your consciousness that nobody can destroy. Once you have access to this level, your karma can be transformed.

In connection with the Mandala Gohonzon this "one heart" (*Ichinen*) is presented in its center as the mantra of Nam-myō-hō-ren-ge-kyō. By chanting daimoku you activate the Buddha nature or the cosmic non-local consciousness deep in your life and begin to unfold this unlimited source of wisdom, health and happiness. The entire mandala therefore shows "all experiences" (*Sanzen*) of transforming your karma and improving your life situation.

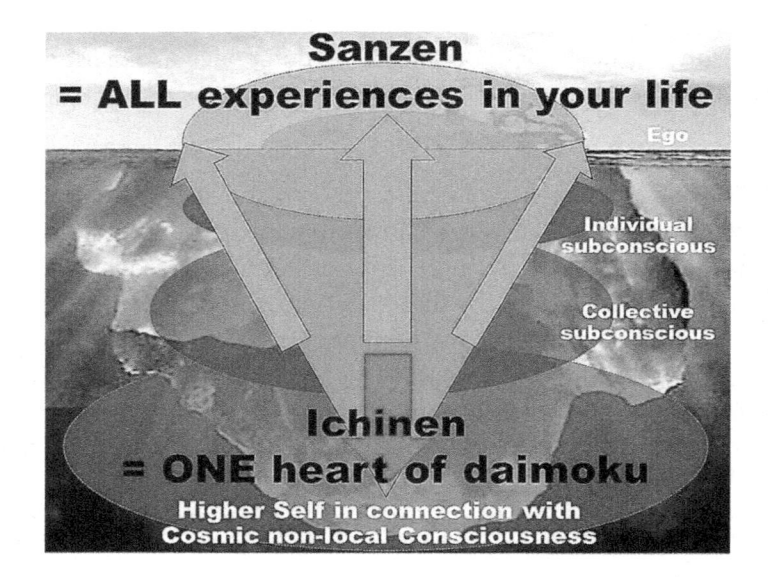

**Sanzen
= ALL experiences in your life**
Ego
Individual subconscious
Collective subconscious
**Ichinen
= ONE heart of daimoku**
Higher Self in connection with
Cosmic non-local Consciousness

Chapter 11

Your subconscious mind is in your body

> Karma cannot be avoided. Karmic energy is returned with the same intensity with which it was generated. Depending on your previous actions, this could create happiness or suffering. Whatever happens, is the result of karma being released, which, no matter how you view the situation, is a good thing and an opportunity for future growth. — Deepak Chopra

Why is karma so persistent?

In order to change our karma and live a happy life, Nichiren established a specific practice to get into touch with the ninth consciousness, the non-local consciousness inherent in our lives. He knew that karma consistently plays a decisive role in our lives and that it is hidden in the deepest layers of our subconscious minds.

Nichiren gave us a very new and specific insight into this mind-body connection. For years I wondered what he meant by saying that the Gohonzon is in the flesh of a believer.

Didn't Nichiren say to Abutsubō, his ardent follower in Sado, that Abutsubō is the Treasure Tower (of the Gohonzon) and the treasure tower is Abutsubō? Isn't he saying here that our body contains the most elevated state of life, the tenth state of life, the state of enlightened consciousness i.e. the state of Buddhahood? And if your body contains the state of Buddhahood, aren't all the other states of life included in the state of Buddhahood? Therefore your body also contains the other nine states of life. This is something that we experience when we have negative emotions, when we are low in energy or ill in any way. We experience anger and joy in a real, physical sense. These are quite visceral, physical states. So is the state of enlightenment. In other words, as Nichiren told us clearly, our body and mind are not just connected, but our body *is* our mind. In this point, it is interesting to see that he is backed up by the results of modern science.

As already mentioned in Chapter 8, research in the field of biology and neuroscience shows that 95% of our programs consist of automatic, unconscious programs, whereas the remaining 5% of programs are conscious and deliberate. When talking about "programs" we mean all the subconscious tendencies towards certain habits, feelings, thoughts, and reaction patterns, which are deeply stored on the physical level in our cells. Thus, our bodies actually act as our "subconscious minds", too. In this sense all the old emotions and habits stored in your body, which is your mind, determine your thoughts and actions, and thus the course of your entire life.

That´s why deliberately "deciding" to feel better with your rational mind usually doesn't work. If you say you want one thing, but you believe something else at a deeper subconscious level, you are blocking yourself from achieving success in that area.

For example, you might tell yourself, "I really want to meet a person I will be happy with." But if at a deep subconscious level you inwardly believe, "That's never going to happen at my age. I'm too old now", then it will be difficult to make this dream a reality. This applies to every area of your life: to the amount of money you want to have, to your health, to your success. Why? It's very simple.

> Your conscious willpower can *never* be stronger than your subconscious mind, which may sabotage your decisions and actions.

We are now going to have a more detailed look at this karmic mechanism according to biologic and neuroscientific aspects, i.e. referring to the memory mechanism of your karmic patterns at the level of your brain cells. This enables us to become more aware of our ways of thinking and feeling so that we can start to change our lives in the ways that we want to, instead of remaining at the mercy of our karma.

Karma is stored on a cellular level

The latest research in biology and neuroscience suggests that even the cells of our body have some form of "consciousness." Some approaches go so far as to claim that our personal identity and our own self-image are mainly based on the programming of our cellular consciousness. This indicates that they are connected with each other by our emotions. We now know that emotion is not locked in our brain; it occurs in every cell of our body. When you pass an examination after having prepared for it for a long time, not only will you have a happy expression on your face, but your whole body will be filled with joy. The positive energy that your body radiates in this case further affects the people around you in an uplifting way.

The late American neuroscientist and pharmacologist Candace Pert (1946-2013) explained that when we feel a certain emotion the brain releases specific neuropeptides across every cell in the body. This information is in the nervous system, the endocrine system and the immune system. We have emotion in our livers and pancreases in the same way as we have emotion in our guts. We don't have a mind and a body as if they were two separated entities. Our body *is* our mind.

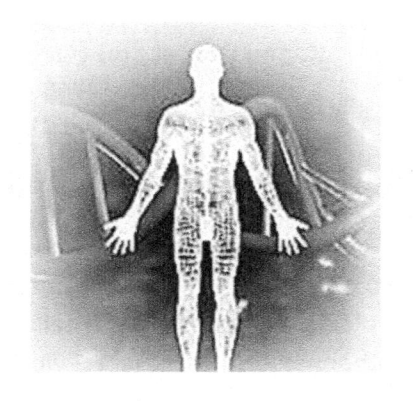

> Your body acts as your mind.
> Your emotion is present in every cell of your body.

When you experience a certain emotion over a period of long time, your body's cells start to build receptors for that specific "neuropeptide wash". This is why we get biologically addicted to this emotion.

Whenever your cells divide, they do so by reproducing the gene that creates same receptors. Thus, if you have been going through a period where you often felt angry, stressed out or anxious, by now your cells have developed receptors that are expecting exactly this emotion. In this case, you have physically conditioned your body to suffer. Your inclination toward a certain emotion builds up a habitual tendency and becomes part of your personality. In this way our karmic tendencies are basically stored in our bodies and now in turn start to condition us.

> Karma basically means your habitual ways of thinking, acting and feeling.

Karma in terms of emotional energy

This in turn has huge consequences for your life since the energy you emanate from within attracts situations and people on the outside. Emotions have a really powerful effect and can affect another person and the larger world. How come? In standard science, emotions are still considered to be only chemistry, but according to Pert emotions are also physics and vibrations. You have receptors in every cell in your body. They are like mini electrical pumps. When the receptor is activated by a matching "molecule of emotion", as Pert puts it, the receptor passes a charge into the cell changes the cell's electrical frequency as well as its chemistry.

Feelings literally alter the electrical frequencies generated by our bodies, producing a nonverbal form of communication with our environment. Pert explained that we're not just little hunks of meat. We're vibrating like a tuning fork – we send out a vibration to other people. We broadcast and receive. Just as our individual cells carry an electrical charge, so does the body as a whole, like an electromagnet generating a field.

Emotions are therefore very important. They are the key for any change. Your emotions leave a huge effect on your environment and on other people, significantly changing the world around you.

According to Pert, the most important indicator for how healthy you'll be is your level of self-esteem. You'll never allow yourself to have more than you feel you deserve, and nobody does this to you: you are doing it to yourself *through* others. You are attracting what you *feel* worthy of having in all parts of your life. Thus, changing your karma implies changing your emotions.

> The emotional energy that you emanate from within attracts situations and people on the outside.

We are addicted to certain emotions

Are you aware of how you habitually think and feel? As mentioned above, your thoughts and feelings cause chemical reactions in the body. After a certain period of time, the body keeps "asking" for these chemical reactions. That's when you start to become addicted to them. You may notice this kind of habitual addiction and attachment very clearly when you try to break through old patterns, such as when trying to give up alcohol or cigarettes, for instance. In the same way we can be addicted to feeling lonely and abandoned, fearful or anxious.

Case study 7: To stop smoking

Unlike today, smoking cigarettes was considered to be calming, easy-going and even cool when I went to University. Originally I had started because smoking cigarettes gave me the feeling of having something to "cling on to" and had a soothing effect on me. Whenever I got nervous or was under stress, I just smoked a cigarette.

When I started chanting daimoku in 1997, however, my attitude towards smoking soon changed. Peter was one of the members of the group I chanted with and who had been very friendly and always supporting me. Suddenly he was diagnosed with lung cancer. I was shocked. Until then, I had presumed that chanting would protect me from getting ill. Now I realized that this was not the case. Peter had been smoking all his life long. His situation showed me that it is essential to take care of your health. I realized that daimoku doesn't stop you from getting ill when you do things that are detrimental to your health.

It hurt me to find out that the doctor had predicted a lot of pain for this group member. However, this turned out to not be the case. The power of daimoku had indeed helped: his wife told us that he died very peacefully and that he did not have the pain the doctors had thought he would have. This was especially astonishing, since they had predicted that he would probably die of suffocation. In the end, he was very much protected and experienced the positive effects of daimoku in his process of dying.

There was another trigger that caused me to stop smoking. At that time one of the members I often chanted together with asked me to take her to a weird exhibition. It was the exhibition of German anatomist Gunther von Hagen, who invented a special technique for preserving biological tissue called "plastination." He uses this technique to preserve human corpses and put them on exhibition. My friend did not have a car at the time. She really urged me to take her to this exhibition because it would be very helpful for her work as a nurse. In the end I agreed to take her there and she convinced me to come along to see the exhibition as well.

Having arrived there, the first thing that really struck me was a real person's lung and next to it another real lung that had belonged to a heavy smoker. In contrast to the first lung, the smoker's lung was actually black. This was a very drastic example of the principle of *cause* and *effect* but it had a very deep impact on me. All of a sudden everything was absolutely real and obvious to me. What was I doing? What causes were I setting for my future life and health? I remembered that my mother had told me that she just wanted to live for ten more years, but it wasn't meant to be. When she was dying, she was craving for life. I wasn't showing appreciation for my life and my health. At that moment I made up my mind to stop smoking. And I did. I stopped from one day to the next. That's when all the hidden feelings emerged that I had been dampening by smoking cigarettes.

I was standing in a queue at McDonalds to get something to drink. Suddenly I had an overwhelming feeling of anger towards the person in front of me, who just could not make up his mind what to get. I could have literally killed him. I was very surprised about the intensity of this feeling and chanted as soon as I got home. Later on I realized how addicted I was to cigarettes in a real physical sense and how frustrated I was due to the lack of nicotine. Every time I felt the urge to smoke I would start chanting immediately and this urge would disappear. After five days those disturbing emotions subsided and I felt I had control over myself again. The chanting had helped me to deeply value my life and to stop a strong habit that had been a very negative cause in my life.

The more that time went on, the less I could stand the smell of cigarette smoke any more. I could see the dull energy of people who were smoking and realized that they were keeping themselves on a low energetic level for as long as they were smoking. The more I increased my energy by chanting **daimoku**, the more I became "allergic" to smoking.

Being addicted to a certain way of thinking

In the same way, it might also be very difficult when you try to give up a certain way of thinking and acting. For example, do you often compare yourself to others? Do you often feel disadvantaged?

Michael told me his story after he had been chanting for some time. He had suddenly become very aware of his own feelings. He told me that he was constantly thinking, "Everyone else got everything that they need from their parents, so they are much better off than me today." If anything went wrong in his life, he was annoyed. If someone he met was very successful, he immediately felt angry, deprived and envious. After a while he became increasingly frustrated and aggressive.

He realized that he reacted like this out of habit and that he was almost addicted to that feeling. Even when everything went well, he began to suddenly argue with his partner and accused her of petty little things. Often he felt annoyed when she did not clean up or when she did not come home exactly at the time that she had said that she would. Deep down he knew that all of this had nothing to do with her or with other people. He knew he was just looking for an occasion to express his inner frustration.

He came to the conclusion that the people in his surroundings just triggered certain feelings that had long been stored within him. He finally realized that his feeling of anger always appeared when he didn't feel respected. He was always reawakening an old feeling. This happened quite often. He could now break through this vicious circle by chanting every time that his old feelings would come up.

In this way, the body of a person who is often annoyed is always asking for the chemical substances that are produced by the body due to these feelings. Have you often felt insecure recently? This may also be a feeling that your cells are "screaming for" again and again.

> We are literally flooding our cells over and over with the same emotions.

Any change or interruption in our usual biochemical condition feels very uncomfortable. When we try to change our habitual feelings, it's like an alcoholic trying to stop drinking. Just about anyone can make you angry at that time.

> We are addicted to a certain feeling from the past.

Exercise 18: What feelings have you become accustomed to?

Are you experiencing any situation that always stirs up the same emotion within you?

_____

Which emotion keeps coming up in your life? How do you tend to react?

_____

Do you feel a lot of anger, fear, anxiety, envy, jealousy, insecurity, unworthiness or powerlessness?

Are you overwhelmed by this feeling?

How would you like to feel instead?

Would you like to feel inspired, confident, optimistic, full of self-love?

Daimoku releases your stored emotions

As mentioned before, your emotions are not the sole product of your brain, but actually stored in the cells of your body. Remember, the body is also part of the subconscious mind! We are all carrying painful emotions of suffering, loss, failure and disappointment within us. If we can´t transform them, these emotions work in the background and can make us ill. However, there is a solution. My experience is that the spiritual practice of chanting **daimoku** causes old, bound energy to be dissolved and released.

> The more often that you evoke positive emotions within yourself by practicing **daimoku**, the more that you can condition your body to create and feel positive emotions.

By doing this, your cells will form more receptors for joy and confidence, and you will automatically feel more of these positive emotions. You stop being dependent on negative emotions and you become free to feel the uplifting emotions of joy, freedom and happiness.

At the beginning of my daimoku practice, I noticed some "victim cells" within me that were constantly looking for respectful recognition of my person by others. After a few years of practicing daimoku I noticed that these cells were starving, as they were no longer given sufficient "victim neuropeptides". I felt more like the creator of my life.

The healing sound frequency of daimoku combined with the frequency of the Gohonzon powerfully combine to clear the body's chakras by releasing pent up energies and emotions that are frequently stuck there. As shown in our book *Nichiren Buddhism 3.0* (see Chapters 7 and 8), our energy measurements clearly revealed that chanting daimoku significantly activates and increases the energy of the body's chakras and strengthen the body's energy field.

This positive effect of practicing daimoku can be demonstrated by comparing two different results of one of the energy measurements. The first picture on the left shows the result of a person who has never meditated or chanted before and whose energy is very disrupted. His energy centers are not aligned and very small. On the contrary, the second picture on the right shows the state of my chakras on a day when I even felt stressed out. The medical staff who took the measurement asked me whether I had been meditating for many years. I told them I had been chanting daimoku for many years. Thus, my chakras remained very centered, aligned and balanced. This shows that daimoku has a balancing effect on our emotions and refills our energy.

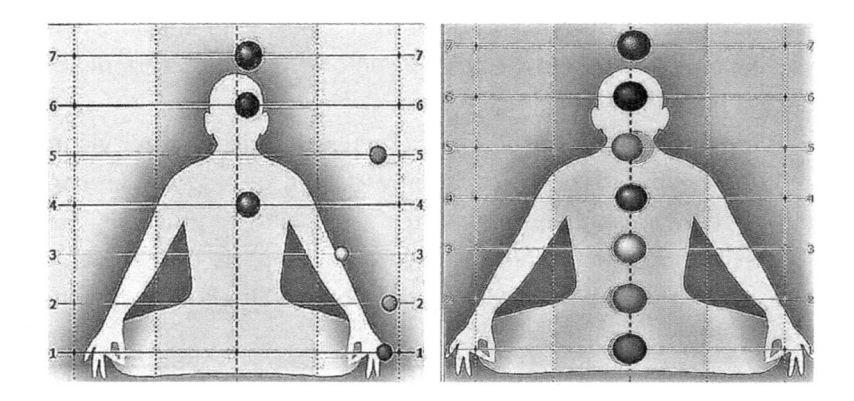

This energy is then available for the realization of a new life. That's why you may start crying when you chant because your old, suppressed feelings come to the surface, which is caused by activating and releasing the blocked energy in your body.

One participant of our daimoku sessions told me that she almost fell sick when an old suppressed feeling soared up while she was chanting. She then went on chanting intensively until she had transformed that feeling. Sometimes it happens to me that for no apparent reason tears rise to my eyes when I chant.

When I am filling my energy field with the positive frequency of daimoku, with joy and happiness, I am literally purging the low vibrations out of me. That means — they're releasing!

Many people told me that they could not understand why they felt so many old emotions during or after chanting. It is important to understand this process.

Let that happen. It's old energy that was stored in your cell-consciousness and that is coming to the surface of your consciousness so that it can go away.

The bound energy that is thereby released no longer weighs on you. You can now let it flow into actively creating a new reality.

Disrupt your emotional addictions

Since the beginning of my practice I realized that worrying, fear and anger were the feelings that often prevented me from reaching my goals and from being happy. After a while I realized that I felt fear or started worrying whenever I thought that my wishes or my goals could not be fulfilled. Whenever things did not turn out the way that I wanted them to, I felt frustrated and started worrying.

All these feelings cause even more worry. That is the feeling you can become addicted to. Sometimes people tell us, "I have chanted so much that I'm almost hoarse, but I still haven't reached my goal." After a while I realized that you can become addicted to reaching your goals. All suffering comes from addiction, from being too attached to the outcome when chanting.

The crucial point in this case is that you are not leaving it up to the Gohonzon to bring about the *how* of the solution. In this case you do not give any space to the greater cosmic consciousness to cooperate and support you. You yourself are in the way. Whenever you are addicted, you worry. In such a moment, it is time to develop deep faith and surrender to the Gohonzon.

All of these feelings of worry, however, never bring to you the things that you want. Quite to the contrary. The feelings of worry and frustration actually repel the things that you want to achieve.

> "Never seek this Gohonzon outside yourself!"

This guidance of Nichiren Daishōnin suggests that you should not seek the solution of your problems outside of yourself, or in all the strategies you apply based on your limited ego consciousness.

Since "the palace of the ninth consciousness" is presented in the Gohonzon, you have just to surrender to the Gohonzon and to trust the power that you are activating by chanting **daimoku**.

Nichiren used to call this attitude of deep trust in your daimoku practice the "strategy of the Lotus Sutra":

> It is the heart that is important. No matter how earnestly Nichiren prays for you, if you lack faith, it will be like trying to set fire to wet tinder. Spur yourself to muster the power of faith. [...] Employ the strategy of the Lotus Sutra before any other.
> *The strategy of the Lotus Sutra (Reply to Shijō Kingo) (1279)*

Chapter 12

The neuroscience of karma

> Life is 10% what happens to you, and 90% how you react to it.

Your karma is stored in your neural networks

Our thoughts, memories, experiences and reactions are stored in our brain as neural networks, as well as in our "mind-bodies". Our brain consists of 100 billion tiny nerve cells called neurons. Each neuron has between 1,000 and 10,000 synapses, which are the connections between one neuron and another. By means of these connections, neurons form innumerable interconnected networks.

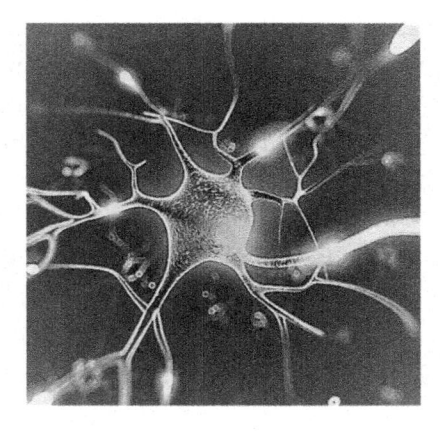

Everything that we have ever experienced so far is, so to speak, stored as a karmic record in these neural networks, including certain emotions connected to your memories. These neural networks are not isolated, but connected to each other. Such connections form complex ideas, memories and emotions.

Each of us has accumulated our own experiences and abilities. What we think, feel and do over and over again leads to the formation of widely branched and hard-wired neural networks. Our personal experiences are stored in these neural networks: how we grew up, our cultural background, our religious beliefs, whether we had many siblings or none at all, what we have experienced with men or women. In our neural networks it is also stored how we eat and drink, how we treat each other, what kind of school education we had or whether we were loved or encouraged by our parents. All of this affects the neural networks in our brain. All these experiences affect how we perceive the world.

Release old traumatic experiences

Do you still remember the coherent "whole brain state" we talked about in Chapter Seven? Every time your brain reorganizes in response to that state you have to let go of the unresolved mental and emotional stuff we all have under the surface, in our subconscious minds. Whether it is unresolved fear, anger, anxiety, sadness, or limiting beliefs, some of this material will be incompatible with the brain's ability to operate at a higher level of functioning and will be resolved.

Research shows that old emotional trauma is resolved once you reach increased coherence in the theta brainwave state. Our measurements have shown that we can increase our theta coherence drastically when chanting daimoku. Thus, you are able to release your old emotional wounds while chanting daimoku.

Whilst chanting for many years, gradually many old painful events became mere neutral memories that did not arouse any strong emotional reaction anymore. For a long time I remembered my brother's mean behavior at the day of my mother's funeral, when he was shouting at me at the cemetery. I vividly remember this terrible scene, which at the time really shocked and emotionally disturbed me. This old feeling used to come up for many years, every time that I thought about that incident. After years of chanting, however, it was nothing but a memory that didn't bother me anymore.

Thus, our emotions play a very significant and decisive role in our daily lives, in the sense that they influence both the body and the mind. In Nichiren Buddhism there is the "principle of the union" or "inseparability of mind and body" (*Shikishin funi*) which is now specifically understood as follows:

> Though mind and body have their own specific functions they are intrinsically connected with each other via emotions that form our basic state of life and influence both our mind and body.

Neurons that fire together wire together

If you focus your mind on worrying, self-criticism and anger, for instance, then your brain will develop neural structures of anxiety, low self-esteem and aggressive reactions towards others. In this case you keep firing your neurons that hold those negative beliefs about yourself. The more you stimulate these neural pathways through feeling those painful emotions, the stronger and more automatic they become. Neuroscientists have the common saying that "neurons that fire together wire together". That´s why after a while we tend to react automatically in a certain way.

For us it is quite normal to react to certain incidents in a certain way. Chanting **daimoku**, however, helps you to interpret any seemingly frightening situation in a new way. It is quite understandable that you may react with anxiety when you lose your job, for example. But even then it is possible to give this incident a new, different meaning when you chant **daimoku**.

For it might not be the fact that you lost your job that is bothering you the most. It may be your own reaction to the job loss and what you think of yourself because of it. The question is: What old neural networks are now being activated and firing together? This is the moment when you think, "I knew I'd never be successful in life".

But it is not the loss of your job that really gets you down, because this could well be the stepping stone to further great development. It is your old self-image that causes you problems.

The question is which neural networks are being activated and are firing together at this very moment? Is the neural network activated where your uncertainty and lack of self-confidence is stored? Or are you able to build a new neural network where stability and self-confidence are activated?

When we practice **daimoku** we can give a *new meaning* to any loss, because it is a matter of experience that the Gohonzon always provides *something better* for us.

In addition, when chanting, we can clearly decide to set a new positive intention, which eventually leads to the formation of a new neural network where self-confidence and trust in the future is stored. This neural network then forms the new template through which we perceive our reality.

The powerful patterns of your emotional reactions

However, it is not just the memories of old events and situations that are stored in our brain. What affects us the most is the emotional content of the old, long forgotten experiences that are deeply encoded in our brains and influence the way we emotionally react to whatever we experience today. These emotional reaction patterns are stored in what neuroscientists call "implicit memory". They are developed, primarily, in the earliest years of your life. They are encoded as non-verbal, non-logical emotional information in the amygdala and other neural structures. So far so good. However, there is one thing that you might not be aware of: They still affect your daily life today.

I have often experienced such automatic reactions. My husband might ask me why one single "idiot" who behaves unfriendly or disrespectful can make me feel upset and get me out of sync, even when ten of my friends or colleagues are showing a lot of appreciation for something that I did, for instance. Normally we cannot consciously decide how we are going to react. But what if you could influence the way you feel and interrupt your automatic response?

The emotional content of your memories

You are usually not aware that old memories are still working in the background of your conscious daily life. They operate on their own, without your conscious intent. Implicit memories are triggered by association, and then arise as pure emotional reactions, not as specific memories of a past event. You don't actually have to remember these "memories" for them to be active. That means you don't have to be actually talking to your mother or father in order to trigger the emotional patterns and the implicit memory of your "mother or father karma".

Have you ever experienced that some seemingly trivial event or behavior of somebody else can trigger such an implicit memory and cause a strong emotional reaction that surprises even yourself?

Case study 8: Projecting old experiences to the present

> One of the neighbors in our street parked right in front of our house even though we had put up a sign with our number plates to deter people from doing that. As soon as I saw it I felt an overwhelming feeling of anger, even hatred. My husband was very surprised about my strong reaction because the situation hadn't bothered him at all.
>
> When I was chanting later on, I realized that my overreaction had something to do with the emotional content of an old, implicit memory of my brother's behavior when I was young. I automatically reacted as though my neighbor had parked his car in front of our house *on purpose, just to annoy me*. This is precisely what my brother used to do. The night before my final exams at college he walked up and down in wooden clogs in his room, which was right above my bed room. He did this *on purpose, just to annoy me*, so that I would not be able to sleep and would not be fit in the morning to take my exams. The anger

and powerlessness associated with this memory had just reared up, triggered by my neighbor's behavior, and suddenly flooded my mind and my body with strong sensations. I felt a strong knot in my stomach. Until then I had not been conscious about feeling resentment, anger or powerlessness towards my brother anymore.

This incident showed me, however, that the old emotional content of my old memories was sometimes still active without me being aware of it. The emotions were stored within me waiting to be triggered by some external event or connotation.

For the next couple of days this neighbor continued to park his car directly in front of our house. I chanted deeply to overcome the feeling of anger and frustration within me. I set the clear intention that this had to stop immediately. I also chanted for him to stop parking there. Then I felt relaxed and did not assign the old feelings of anger to that event anymore. Surprisingly enough, he has indeed stopped parking in front of our house ever since that day and began parking his car along the hedge of our next door neighbor. It was mystical!

Your brain is a record of your past

As long as you do not build new neural pathways of positive states and thoughts, your inherent memories will continue to plague you. Your existing pathways will only get stronger.

> Without building new neural connections
> you cannot set new causes and react differently.

A neurofeedback expert I talked to told me that if you continuous think anxious thoughts, for example, your brain literally takes on the shape of an anxious person. But how can we stop these automatic responses? How can we reverse this process?

The latest research shows that the brain continues to change and produce neurons throughout life. This "neuroplasticity" means that even when we are old, we can change the way that we respond to negative thoughts, and these responses will eventually change how we react to others permanently.

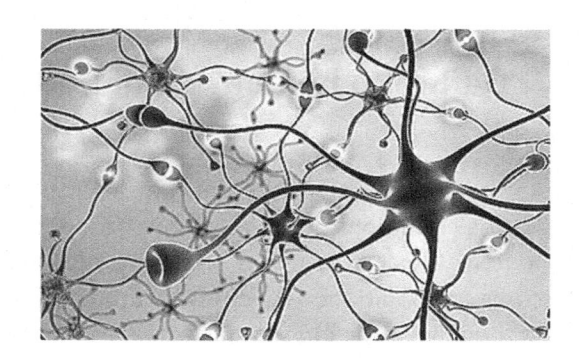

Neurons in the brain transferring information among each other

The question is how to do that. After many years of daimoku practice and a lot of research into the latest results of neuroscience, I realized that somehow you must first be able to *interrupt* this vicious circle of your automatic emotional responses before you can focus on anything new, and therefore start to form new neural pathways.

Nichiren tells us that we can *break through* our karmic patterns by chanting daimoku. And indeed, this is what our measurements revealed.

Chapter 13

Daimoku is a powerful pattern breaker

> Karma creates the future, but it is also an echo from the past. Karma conditions our mind through memory, desire and imagination. Most people are prisoners of karma, because it becomes a conditioned reflex and produces predictable outcomes in their lives. The goal of enlightenment is to break the shackles of karma.
> – Deepak Chopra

Daimoku interrupts emotional addictions

As highlighted in the last two chapters, our emotional addictions are stored in our subconscious minds, i.e. in both our neural networks in our brains and on a cellular level in our bodies. This is the reason why we can't easily change our karmic patterns of thinking and feeling by just deciding to do so with our conscious minds alone. And this is also the reason why chanting **daimoku** to the Gohonzon is necessary for getting access to cosmic consciousness and freeing us from our emotional addictions. **Daimoku** interrupts and transforms these emotions that are holding you in their grip. The more often you release these "emotional addictions" while chanting **daimoku**, the easier you can give them up completely. This is releasing your karma.

Now, what if you could influence the way you feel and interrupt your automatic response? That's exactly what you can do, by chanting **daimoku**. Even after only five minutes you can feel different about anything that bothers you.

Your thoughts are far more often concerned with reviewing the past and rehearsing the future than being completely in the present. The present moment, the now, is the only moment in which you really live. The past is over and the future hasn't come about yet. Only the present is available for you.

As we mentioned before, our personality consists of 95% of unconscious thoughts, automatic programs, recurring habits, emotional reactions and engrained ways of thinking and acting. These routine programs have an effect on your mental, physical, energetic, biochemical and emotional states and keep you stuck in the past. You will remember that your brain is a record of your past. As long as we live under the influence of our familiar emotions, our body is actually living in the past. As long as we are captured in these karmic patterns, we are just like a hamster in a wheel.

There is only one way to get off this hamster wheel: We must be able to consciously interrupt the patterns by having access to the karma-free zone of the unified field of pure consciousness where your karmic causes have lost their effect. By doing so, we can transcend karma and become independent of it by breaking its hold of us. This enables us to stop living on the low frequency of the latent memories that anchored us to the emotions of the past. In this state we become aware of our own patterns of feeling, talking and acting.

At some point I realized that we have to stop talking in a self-limiting way. This required me to interrupt my unconscious patterns every day, in order to elevate my energy on a daily basis and adjust it to the frequency of a new future.

Whenever we increase our energy and our frequency by chanting daimoku, the feeling of separation between us and the unified field of consciousness gets weaker. By chanting daimoku we close the gap between our individual conditioned consciousness and the pure consciousness of the unified field as deeply as we can. This happens whenever we deeply connect and surrender to the Gohonzon.

Our measurements have shown that you generate more coherent theta and delta brainwaves while chanting which are supposed to connect you to this unified field of pure consciousness. I have often experienced that the less separated we are from this field, the quicker our new future emerges. For every time you change your energy by chanting daimoku, you are reorganizing your environment in a way that suits your new future. Everything that does not vibrationally fit any more to your new future will disappear. Don´t be worried. This is just your past wanting to leave.

It makes a significant difference in terms of the effect of daimoku when you leave everything old that belongs to the past behind you and open yourself up for everything new that is unfolding in your life. That is the decision for your new future that you deliberately make in front of the Gohonzon. Every time that you chant daimoku with this understanding you will naturally develop and establish the understanding that the practice of daimoku represents the foundation of your new life. This simple possibility to be able to chant is very joyful, because you can always start your life anew with great confidence.

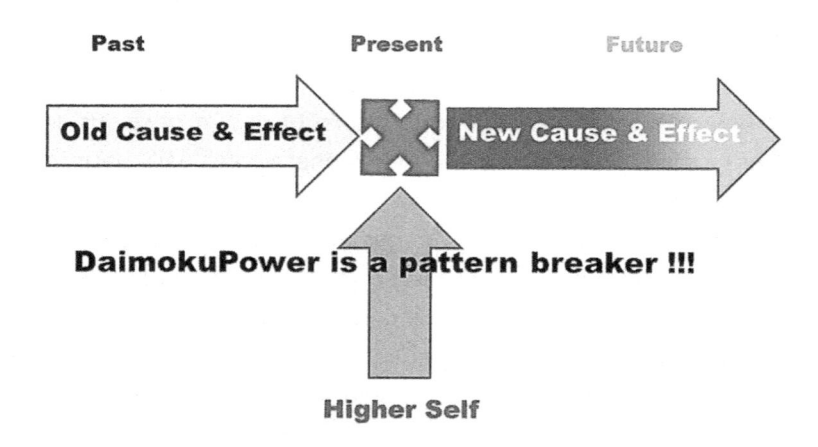

Past   **Present**   **Future**

Old Cause & Effect → ← **New Cause & Effect**

DaimokuPower is a pattern breaker !!!

↑

Higher Self

You are not only confronted with your karmic conditioning when you chant daimoku. In your daily life you are constantly challenged to recognize your karmic patterns and to break through those causal chains that make you suffer, and to immediately transform each life situation. In both cases, you are using the power of daimoku as a "pattern breaker":

This aspect of your daimoku practice is extremely important, and can break through your persistent karmic patterns even in concrete neuroscientific terms. For this purpose we undertook some further brainwave measurement while we were chanting that confirmed that daimoku indeed functions as a real "pattern breaker".

Brainwave measurement while chanting together

We had often experienced that chanting together in a group generates a powerful dynamic. We wanted to find out if this dynamic would show itself in a brain scan. In this case we decided to take a QEEG measurement at four points of Yukio's head, which were selected by our neurofeedback expert.

We measured Yukio's brainwaves in three stages in order to check the respective changes that may occur while we were chanting:

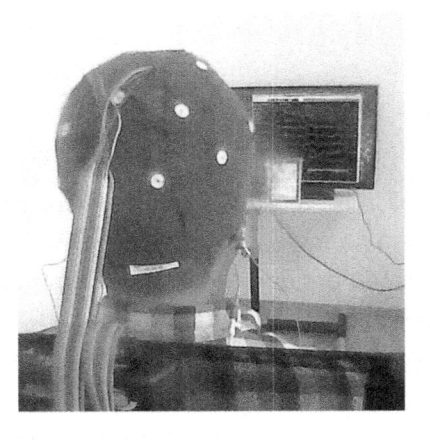

QEEG-Measurement of brainwaves

❶ Yukio remained sitting in his chair doing a number of deep breathing exercises for about 4 minutes.
❷ He started to chant daimoku towards the compact Gohonzon in front of him for about another 4 minutes.

❸ Then Susanne joined him to chant together for about 10 minutes.

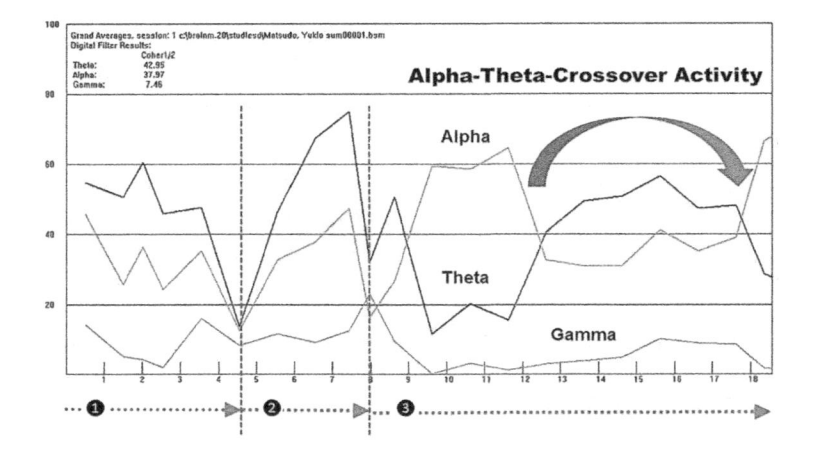

Alpha-Theta-Crossover Activity

During the first phase, when he was calmly breathing in and out (❶), the theta brainwaves were already more active than the alpha brainwaves. This means that Yukio´s brain seemed to be balanced enough to become calm and relaxed in a very short time. As soon as he started to chant **daimoku** (❷), there was a huge increase in theta brainwaves accompanied by an additional increase in alpha brainwaves. According to our neurofeedback expert, such an increase certainly indicates an altered state of consciousness emerging during meditation.

Then I joined him in chanting (❸). During this phase of chanting together, the measurements taken of Yukio´s brain showed a striking pattern concerning the holistic functioning of a brain. During this phase, alternating alpha-theta patterns occurred in Yukio's frontal cerebral area. As you can see on the chart, an enhanced alpha pattern emerges and is then crossed by a theta pattern.

This "alpha-theta crossover pattern" is a significant indicator of how the different brain areas communicate with each other. In this case, the two brain hemispheres are balanced and in unison, "speaking together" in a more harmonious way.

> Measuring Yukio´s brainwaves with a QEEG showed that during the phase when we were chanting together a certain pattern emerged, the so-called "alpha-theta crossover", known as a "pattern breaker" in neurofeedback therapy.

The clinical application of the alpha-theta crossover

The neurofeedback expert who undertook the measurement while we were chanting was astonished at the result. Since he considered chanting daimoku to be a meditative practice, he only expected a certain increase of alpha brainwaves, suggesting a calm and peaceful state of mind as is mostly the case with many other forms of meditative practices. The measurement of Yukio's brainwaves, however, immediately showed the trancelike state of the so-called alpha-theta amplitude crossover where alpha waves and theta waves, which signify deep relaxation, are elevated: frequencies found to promote a healing state that could be used to treat many things, from alcoholism and drug addiction to depression and anxiety.

Our neurofeedback expert, who had been engaged in treating patients who had been suffering from substance addiction for a long time, explained to us that the neurofeedback training he offered was aimed to exactly generate this kind of alpha-theta crossover. This therapy intends to transform unpleasant negative emotions such as anxiety, tension, anger, depression, and the feeling of uncertainty into pleasant emotions such as confidence, wholeness and relaxation.

The clinical effectiveness of the alpha-theta crossover neurofeedback training was first demonstrated with military veterans who were treated for their alcohol addiction. They normally experience an increase in their respective level of stress hormones when they try to completely stay off alcohol during their treatment. Drinking alcohol is often used to escape from an unpleasant and uneasy feeling, accompanied by some fast and restless brain activity in a high beta brainwave state. Thus, people often drink alcohol because alcohol slows down the increased brainwave activity caused by excessive anxiety. The same effect, however, is achieved by the alpha-theta crossover EEG-feedback training, because it normalizes the brainwave activity by slowing down one's brainwaves and thus correcting the slow brainwave activity deficit.

EEG measurements of combat veterans with some form of post-traumatic stress disorder regularly show an increase in beta brainwave activity and a significant decrease in alpha brainwave activity. Therefore it is essential to find a way to slow down the brainwave activity of patients suffering from post-traumatic stress disorder (PTSD).

This kind of neurofeedback therapy to treat alcoholism has subsequently also been applied to treat various forms of post-traumatic stress disorder (PTSD). The alpha-theta crossover state allows the repressed events that have caused the post-traumatic stress to surface to consciousness and be processed, ending the hold it once had over the patient.

Likewise, the pattern interrupts any addiction-like desire in addicts and puts their brains in such a relaxed and harmonious state that the addiction is soothed.

Our neurofeedback expert confessed to us that it usually takes his addiction patients a very long time to train and develop this wholesome pattern of an alpha-theta crossover in his neurofeedback training. He was very surprised that chanting daimoku had caused the alpha-theta crossover to occur in only a few minutes.

Now we were even more convinced that any unpleasant emotion can be interrupted and transformed by a deep and focused practice of chanting daimoku in front of the Gohonzon.

> Chanting daimoku can put you in the brainwave state of an alpha-theta crossover, which is a pattern breaker that enables you to break your emotional addiction and allows you to positively influence how you feel.

Your intention is already realized

According to meditation researcher and neuroscientist Joe Dispenza, this alternating alpha-theta pattern in the frontal-cerebral area represents a very specific state of consciousness in which the intention that you have at this moment is experienced as if it has already happened. Such a special pattern also implies that the intention that you have at this moment is experienced with a strong certainty and conviction.

This experience is accompanied by the emotion that we feel when we get exactly what we have wished for. Yukio reported that he experienced a flowing sensation with a rising feeling of joy and a strong sense of happiness during our phase of chanting together. At that moment he could also hold a clear intention, feeling that his intention was "carried" by the power of daimoku.

From alpha to theta to delta

Measuring our brainwaves while chanting had clearly shown that daimoku is indeed a pattern breaker. According to Dispenza, you are connecting to universal consciousness whenever your brainwaves are in a coherent theta or delta state. Just enjoy the flow of life and trust in it. Whenever you are connected to universal life force, you can shift away old, non-serving beliefs and replace their energy with that of new, more empowering beliefs. That happens every time your brainwaves are in the theta state while chanting.

This is why the theta brainwave state is so important, as it aligns your subconscious mind to the frequency of growth and change. It opens your mind for positive change and allows you to directly access your subconscious mind in order to install new beliefs and images. The delta brainwave state takes us a step even further. It gives us the ability to change beliefs from the spiritual level of pure consciousness.

You can feel it when you are deeply connected to the Gohonzon. You can focus on new emotions that you want to experience and create a new vision of your life. In that state I feel a presence within me and around me that is guiding my thoughts and feelings.

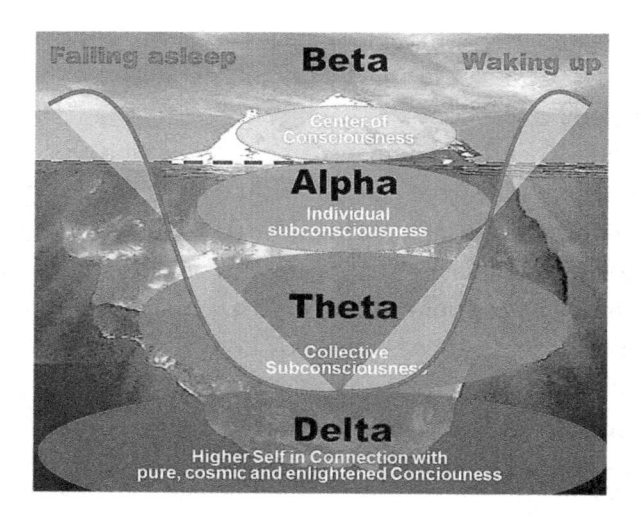

Emotionally living in the future

Dispenza raises one important question whenever you try to create a new state of life and whenever you want to realize your vision. "Can I teach my body how the future is going to feel?"

Whenever I do this, I am sending out the exact signals that are causing events to enter my life that correspond to this vision.

Exercise 19: Can you feel your new vision?

Surrender any old feelings of unworthiness, powerlessness or anger to the Gohonzon and get into a new state of being while chanting.

As soon as you feel inspiration, joy and freedom, find a clear vision of what you would like to experience in the future.

Ask yourself a simple question: "What would it be like to be healthy?" "What would it be like to be wealthy?" "What would it be like to be in love?" "What would it be like to have wonderful friends?" "What would it be like to be fit?"

Keep this picture in mind while chanting. Make this vision the blueprint for your future.

How would you feel, think and act in your new life?

_____

_____

_____

According to Dispenza, our body as our subconscious mind cannot distinguish between an actual experience in life that evokes an emotion, and an emotion that exists only in our mind. If we are able to practice the emotional condition before the actual experience, then we are already moving toward this future. The measurement of Yukio's brain frequencies has shown that we can do just that when we are chanting.

Exercise 20: Set your vision for the upcoming day

While chanting in the morning, think about the intentions that you set throughout your day.

Are you intending to enjoy what you are doing?

_____

To be effective and get things done?

_____

Or to just get through the day?

_____

Are you intending to achieve and accomplish your goals, or to just avoid negative outcomes?

_____

Are you intending to really feel good today?

_____

What are your concrete intentions for the day?

_____

Do you have the intention to lead a healthy life style?

_____

Do you have the intention to focus on and complete what you are doing?

_____

Do you have the intention to have a good relationship with your partner?

Polishing your mirror day and night

To use chanting daimoku as a "pattern breaker" in any situation is one important factor in overcoming difficulties and becoming happy. Breaking through your old karmic patterns of thinking, feeling and behaving also means to cleanse your consciousness and your emotional state of life at the same time.

> The same applies to a Buddha as well as to an ordinary being. When deluded, one is called an ordinary being, but when enlightened, one is called a Buddha. This is similar to a tarnished mirror that will shine like a jewel when polished. A mind now clouded by the illusions of the innate darkness of life is like a tarnished mirror, but when polished, it is sure to become like a clear mirror, reflecting the essential nature of phenomena and the true aspect of reality. Arouse deep faith, and diligently polish your mirror day and night. How should you polish it? Only by chanting Nam-myō-hō-ren-ge-kyō.
> *On Attaining Buddhahood in This Lifetime (1255)*

Cleansing your consciousness in this way is quite a natural process, as Nichiren indicated when he compared this process with polishing a mirror. He pointed out that cleaning your mind should be a constant activity and not something you do only once in a while. Nichiren himself saw the necessity of cleaning your mind "day and night" with the power of daimoku.

As emphasized on several occasions, reciting the mantra of Nam-myō-hō-ren-ge-kyō in front of the Gohonzon is the crucial starting point for your efforts to design your life in an innovative way.

Under all circumstances, you can chant **daimoku** with the deep intention to activate and unfold your highest potential.

When you hold such a strong determination, you may often be confronted with your own tendency of wanting to stay lazy and comfortable. Your old conditioning may try to resist any form of renewal and may try to pull you down. On the outside, obstacles and difficulties may arise that give you the impression that you are stuck. However, none of these are stronger than the power of **daimoku,** which serves as a "pattern breaker" to overcome any difficult situation and to put your new vision into practice.

Therefore Nichiren gives us the clear guidance to chant **daimoku** not only in front of the Gohonzon, but also in any situation that may arise in our daily lives.

> Arouse deep faith, and diligently polish your mirror day and night!   – Nichiren

Bibliography

Alexander, Eben: *Proof of Heaven, A Neurosurgeon´s Journey into the Afterlife*, Simon and Schuster Paperbacks, New York, 2012.

Broers, Dieter: *Gedanken erschaffen Realität – Die Gesetze des Bewusstseins*, München, 2013.

Chopra, Deepak, *Das Tor zu vollkommenem Glück – Ihr Zugang zum Energiefeld der unendlichen Möglichkeiten*, Knaur Verlag München, 2004.

Davidson, Richard and Begley, Sharon: *Warum regst du dich so auf? Wie die Gehirnstruktur unsere Emotionen bestimmt*, Wilhelm Goldmann Verlag, München, 2016.

Dispenza, Joe: *Breaking the habit of being yourself – How to lose your mind and create a new one*, Hayhouse UK Ltd, 2012.

Dispenza, Joe: *Du bist das Placebo.Bewusstsein wird Materie*, Koha-Verlag GmbH, Burgrain, 2014.

Dürr, Hans-Peter: *Geist, Kosmos und Physik*, Crotona Verlag, Amerang, 2010.

Dürr, Hans-Peter: *Es gibt keine Materie*, Crotona Verlag, Amerang, 2012

Fannin, Jeffrey: *Understanding brainwaves*, White-Paper.
https://thoughtgenius.com/wp-content/uploads/2015/10/

Fannin, Jeffrey and Williams, Robert: *What neuroscience reveals about the nature of business.*
http://www.newagewellnessworld.com/uploads/9/9/0/9/9909815/

Farwell, Larry: *How Consciousness Commands Matter*, Fairfield, Iowa, 1999.

Fannin, Jeffrey and Williams, Robert: *Leading edge neuroscience reveals significant correlations between beliefs, the whole-brain-state, and psychotherapy,* https://psych-k.com/wp-content/uploads/2013/10/FanninWilliams.CQ-copy.pdf

Hanson, Rick: *Buddha´s brain –the practical neuroscience of happiness, love and wisdom*, New Harbinger Publications, Oakland, 2009.

Harris, Bill: *Thresholds of the mind*, Centerpointe Press, Oregon, 2002.

Haynes, John-Dylan: *Unconscious decisions in the brain*,
https://www.mpg.de/research/unconscious-decisions-in-the-brain

Hoelzel, Britta. Ott, Ulrich: *Meditationsforschung: Neuroanatomische Befunde.* https://www.arbor-verlag.de/files/MeditationForschung_%20HoelzelOtt.pdf

Huether, Gerald: *Es muss unter die Haut,* https://www.freitag.de/autoren/der-freitag/es-muss-unter-die-haut

Ikeda, Daisaku: *Das Prinzip Hoffnung, Goshovorlesungen,* Fata Morgana Verlag, Berlin 2010.

Ikeda, Daisaku, and Mogi, Ken'ichiro: 池田大作×茂木健一郎　往復書簡（第一信から第四信まで）『中央公論』2010 年 4 月号
Dialogue on Science and Religion, Chūōkōron, 2010.
https://ameblo.jp/rebotco5102/entry-12216958881.html

Koch, Christof: *Bewusstsein: Bekenntnisse eines Hirnforschers,* Springer Verlag Berlin-Heidelberg, 2013.

Kochte, Esther: *Theta Floating. Aktiviere das spirituelle Potenzial deines Zellbewusstseins und erschaffe dich neu,* Scorpio Verlag, Berlin, München, 2011.

Korotkov, Konstantin: *Human Energy Field, Study with GDV Bioelectrography,* Fair Lawn, NJ USA, 2002.

Liebermann, Matthew: *Social: Why our brains are wired to connect.* Oxford University Press, Oxford, 2013.

Lipton, Bruce: *Intelligente Zellen – Wie Erfahrungen unsere Gene steuern,* Burgrain, 10. Aufl., 2006.

Littlefair, Sam: *Leading neuroscientists and Buddhists agree: "Consciousness is everywhere",* https://www.lionsroar.com/christof-koch-unites-buddhist-neuroscience-universal-nature-mind/

McTaggart, Lynn: *Das Nullpunktfeld – Auf der Suche nach der kosmischen Ur-Energie,* München, 2007.

McTaggart, Lynn: *The Bond – Wie in unserer Quantenwelt alles mit allem verbunden ist,* München 2011.

McTaggert, Lynn: *Intention- mit Gedankenkraft die Welt verändern.* VAK Verlags GmbH, Freiburg, 2007.

Matsudo, Yukio and Matsudo-Kiliani, Susanne: *Durchbruch mit DaimokuPower – Einführung in den Nichiren-Buddhismus,* Norderstedt, 2012.

Matsudo, Yukio: *Nichiren, der Ausübende des Lotos-Sutra,* DPI Publishing, 2017 (2004).

Ott, Ulrich: *Meditation für Skeptiker,* München, O. W. Barth, 2010.

Peniston, Eugene G.: *Alpha-Theta Brainwave Neuro-Feedback for Vietnam Veterans with CombatRelated Post-Traumatic Stress Disorder*, http://charleston.braincoretherapy.com/wp-content/uploads/2014/01/PENISTON-PTSD.pdf

Pert, Candace B.: *Everything you need to know to feel good*, Hay House, London, 2007.

Pert, Candace B.: *Molecules of emotion – the science behind mind-body medicine*, Touchstone, New York, 1999.

Taylor, Jill Bolte: *My stroke of insight – a brain scientist's personal journey*, Hodder and Stoughton, London, 2008.

Van Lommel, Pim: *Endloses Bewusstsein. Neue medizinische Fakten zur Nahtoderfahrung*, Patmos Verlag der Schwabenverlag AG, Ostfildern, 6. Auflage 2012

Warnke, Ulrich: *Quantenphilosophie und Spiritualität – Der Schlüssel zu den Geheimnissen des menschlichen Seins*, München, 2011.

Warnke, Ulrich: *Quantenphilosophie und Interwelt – Der Zugang zur verborgenen Essenz des menschlichen Wesens*, München, 2013.

About the authors

Susanne Matsudo-Kiliani, PhD

University degree as translator for English and Spanish, PhD in Translation Studies and Religious Studies specializing in Buddhism, Heidelberg University. Certified trainer for Intercultural Competence in International Business.

Dr. Matsudo-Kiliani has been practicing Nichiren Buddhism since 1998 and has experienced many beneficial transformations in her life, which still continue. As a passionate practitioner she has been engaged in building a bridge between Buddhist practice and modern sciences that are now integrating energy and consciousness.

From 2014-2017 she was a member of the council of the German Buddhist Union (DBU e. V.) and acted as representative for interreligious dialogue at a federal level for a better mutual understanding among different religions.

Yukio Matsudo, PhD

PhD in Philosophy and post-doc qualification for professorship (Habilitation) in the subjects of Japanese Buddhism and Comparative Religions, Heidelberg University.

After receiving his post-doc qualification, he was active as a lecturer at

Heidelberg University on the subjects of Japanese Buddhism and Comparative Religions from 2001-2014.

Dr. Matsudo has been practicing Nichiren Buddhism intensively since 1976 and was a top leader of SGI Germany at a federal level until 2001. He has supported hundreds of people in their practice. This way he could also gain many concrete and important experiences.

SGI-President Ikeda asked him personally to found and run as Director of Research *the European Centre of the Institute of Oriental Philosophy* (IOP) in Taplow Court, UK. In this period from 1990-2000, based on the modern, humanistic and open-minded approach of Daisaku Ikeda, he developed an innovative understanding of Nichiren Buddhist teachings and published a number of books and articles in Japanese, German and English.

Today, Dr. Matsudo is engaged in building a bridge between Buddhism, Western philosophy and new scientific disciplines. As an expert in Nichiren Buddhist Studies he is also active in a research group in Japan, in which prominent scholars are represented from all main denominations of Nichiren schools including Soka Gakkai (IOP).